Materia Prima

Selected Poems of
Amanda Berenguer

Edited by

Kristin Dykstra and Kent Johnson

Translated by

Gillian Brassil, Anna Deeny Morales,

Kristin Dykstra, Kent Johnson,

Urayoán Noel, Jeannine Marie Pitas,

Mónica de la Torre, Alex Verdolini

MATERIA PRIMA: Selected Poems of Amanda Berenguer
© The Estate of Amanda Berenguer, 2019

Translation © Gillian Brassil, Anna Deeny Morales, Kristin Dykstra, Kent Johnson, Urayoán Noel, Jeannine Marie Pitas, Mónica de la Torre, Alex Verdolini, 2019

Introduction and Note on the Translations © Kristin Dykstra and Kent Johnson, 2019

Preface © Roberto Echavarren, 2019

Interview © Silvia Guerra, 2019

Published with the kind permission of Álvaro Díaz Berenguer and the Estate of Amanda Berenguer.

The editors and publisher of this collection are grateful to the following journals for publishing previous versions of these translations: *Golden Handcuffs Review*, *The Claudius App*, *The Harvard Review Online*, *Almost Island*, *Mandorla: New Writing from the Americas / Nueva escritura de las Américas*, and *Eleven Eleven*. Several poems also appear in the anthology *Hotel Lautréamont: Contemporary Poetry from Uruguay* from Shearsman. The publisher would like to thank Denise Milstein and Ignacio Bajter for archival assistance.

Lost Literaure Series № 24

ISBN 978-1-946433-06-0
First Edition, Second Printing, 2019

Ugly Duckling Presse
The Old American Can Factory
232 Third Street, № E-303
Brooklyn, NY 11215
www.uglyducklingpresse.org

Distributed by SPD/Small Press Distribution, Inpress Books (UK), and Raincoast Books (Canada) via Coach House Books

Design and typesetting by Cassidy Batiz, Sarah Lawson, and Don't Look Now!
The type is Recta

Books printed offset and bound at Thomson-Shore
Cover printed offset by Prestige Printing
Cover stock and fly leaf are Mohawk Keaykolour

This book was made possible, in part, by a generous grant from the National Endowment for the Arts, and by the continued support of the New York State Council on the Arts.

Table of Contents

Editors' Introduction

> Sketch—ass peeking from narrow basket,
> a little man bent over the basket whacks at it
> with mandolin—there's something lodged between
> the buttocks (honeycomb of bees?)
>
> —Amanda Berenguer (from "The Asses of Bosch")

The bizarre ekphrasis constituting "The Asses of Bosch," a long poem by Amanda Berenguer (1921-2010), alerts us to the Uruguayan writer's startling range. No two books from her impressive career—more than six decades long—sound the same. Even more exciting: Berenguer was capable of sustained focus across complete collections, but also capable of sudden delightful transformation within them. "The Asses of Bosch" was probably composed sometime after her eightieth year and appears, incongruously enough, within a final collection that reads, for the greater part, as Berenguer's most equably serene, lyrical work.

Born in Montevideo, Uruguay in 1921, and a lifelong resident of the capital, Berenguer saw her first book of poetry published in that city in 1940. She led a life dedicated to literature, producing a stream of books, most often poetry collections, while participating in events and publication projects with her contemporaries. Critics consistently list her as one of the key figures of the country's "Generation of 1945." This loosely defined group is comprised of intellectuals and creative writers who got their start at roughly the same time and worked in a variety of genres. Among the most common qualities attributed to them are an internationalist frame of view and a vibrant openness to experimentation. Berenguer's poetry amply exemplifies these principles. She navigates and tacks weirdly between Apollonian reason and Dionysian ecstasy—few poets anywhere have been able to embody the dichotomy with such cool.

In this anthology, one experiences her fascination with cosmology and non-orientable objects in geometry, such as the Möbius strip and the Klein bottle. These objects are displayed in our selections from *Prime Matter / Materia Prima* and *The Green Bottle / La botella verde*. Critic and poet Luis Bravo is one of a number of knowledgeable writers from the Southern Cone to pinpoint poems from *Materia Prima* as groundbreaking moments in Berenguer's unique poetics of time and space. For Bravo, Materia Prima marks Berenguer's "definitive liftoff" into her own poetic zone. Two poems in particular, "Magellanic Clouds" and "Möbius Strip," testify to that development, presenting Berenguer's surveys of the multiplicities and rela-tivities of embodied mind.[1] Whether through quotidian, physical action, or near-mystical contemplative stasis, she travels through manifold dimensions of percep-tion and understanding. In this respect, Bravo observes, *Materia Prima* becomes the key antecedent to the paradoxically immobile journeys in her 1987 collection, *La dama de Elche / The Lady of Elche*.

We have also gathered excerpts that represent her experiments with the concrete, visual elements and dimensions of poetry. These poems tend to be divided into two groups. The first set features pieces dated to the early 1970s and published in the book *Composition of Place / Composición de lugar* (1976), from which we include excerpts. Other visual poems appeared later in the same decade and have been published in more than one configuration. We include a sequence under the title of "Arena" (Sand), which was first printed in 1978. Berenguer's visual poetry can be placed alongside famous examples from Brazil and the River Plate region for chronological and geographical reasons. Yet as translator and poet Urayoán Noel concluded from working with the pieces here, Berenguer, in her remarkable po-em-objects, makes contributions all her own.

Objective specificity and phenomenological tracking continues, variously, in her later work. Her precise, sensual still-lifes in the collection *Identity of Certain Fruits / Identidad de ciertas frutas*, though reminiscent of Neruda's odes in their perceptual and figural intensities, represent a different, and differently vivid, relationship to the visualization of form.

Then there are Berenguer's hilarious, aphoristic notations in excerpts from *With the Tiger Among My Things / Con el tigre entre las cosas*. While editing this anthology, we were stunned to learn that *Con el tigre entre las cosas* was somehow never pub-lished in its own day. Instead it was retrieved much later and added to *Constelación del navío / Ship Constellation*, a huge anthology spanning her career, published in Montevideo in 2002 (though she still had more new writing to come). The mastery of humor and sardonic irony—turned here, in significant measure, towards themes of gender—adds yet more complexity to Berenguer's performances.

She displays a striking command of language and awareness of the senses throughout *The Lady of Elche*, named after a controversial statue that is sometimes taken as the earliest expression of Iberian identity. In this award-winning book, each text achieves a characteristic density, its confluence of sensual experience building on the exquisite attention to visual perception she had previously developed in

---

1   Luis Bravo, "Amanda Berenguer: El texto vivo"

Identity of Certain Fruits. Meanwhile the body's ineluctable presence and transformation, a major theme throughout Berenguer's work, anchors the poems. As Bravo suggests, *The Lady of Elche* succeeds in portraying paradoxically "immobile" journeys of bodies through modernity.

In *The Green Bottle*, Berenguer continues to work out her fascination with peculiar geometric objects—in this case a serial meditation on the Klein bottle. It is a non-orientable object like the Möbius strip, but in fact the bottle is even stranger, for it is not only non-orientable, it also has no boundary; and though it appears to have an "inside," it actually does not. "Reality sheathed within the tube of / reality, I quietly consider / the slight error of transparency," she writes, setting out to ponder the paradoxes of wild form in a building crescendo of precise but mysterious aphorisms. The non-orientable "object" of the series becomes, no less, the unruly, contorting surface of perception and thought proper, whose impossible "inside" poetry seeks to fathom, even if it ultimately falls short.

Also excerpted here is the late collection *Keeper of the Flame / La cuidadora del fuego*, compiled by her friend and fellow poet Roberto Echavarren. Berenguer passed away before she could see it to print. Openly tuned to Emily Dickinson's prosodic concisions and cuts, Berenguer employs the dash as device. She creates a reflective survey of her immediate surrounds and their attendant mythologies, including the poetic legacy of Uruguayan-born Isidore-Lucien Ducasse (a.k.a. France's Comte de Lautréamont, author of the scandalous and pivotal *Les Chantes de Maldoror* and *Poésies*).

How did Amanda Berenguer come to have such a range? To begin with the broadest strokes, her Generation of '45 lived through a series of momentous events and movements that influenced their conversations and thought. Bravo highlights the intensity of the Spanish Civil War and the Second World War, the impact of existential philosophy, questions regarding the political commitment of the artist, Socialist Realism, and a collapse of humanist values—all folding into an immediate and powerful experience of disillusionment with the collapse of democracy in Uruguay. By 1972, internal conflicts raged across the nation, marked by an urban guerrilla movement with significant popular support. 1976 saw a military coup followed by the imprisonment, torture, and disappearance of thousands of Uruguayans associated with opposition, whether violent or peaceful. The military-guided government lasted well into the 1980s and succeeded in demanding immunity for its crimes when democratic presidential elections were reinstituted. Berenguer's poetry forms against these direct and indirect invocations of unresolved violence that are the backdrop to much of her work.

Berenguer's career demonstrates the rewards of insistent, rigorous innovation over the course of decades. In 1944, just four years after the appearance of her first book of poetry, Berenguer married the influential intellectual José Pedro Díaz. They used a garage in Montevideo to house equipment for a small, independent press named La Galatea from 1945 to 1961, publishing works by others as well as four poetry collections by Berenguer. Their long partnership often receives mention in overviews of the Generation of '45, and there is no doubt that Berenguer's work was stimulated during this period by the literary milieu she and her husband helped foster. Family also surfaces as a topic in some of her writing, justifying some degree of critical attention—for example, in *The Lady of Elche*, influential because it won recognition in Spain as well as Uruguay, Berenguer depicts her family members through prisms of classical mythology. Díaz, their children, and sundry ancestors appear in trippy juxtaposition to the ancient past of the Iberian Peninsula and the contemporary geometries of New York City, which she visited in 1979.

The couple would always remain engaged in various aspects of cultural life, sometimes circulating together but also independently. In addition to their early small-press activity, for example, they regularly participated in gatherings hosted by exiled Spanish writer José Bergamín from the late 1940s into the mid-'50s. When Berenguer and Díaz traveled to Europe in 1950/51 and again in 1971, they took the opportunity to meet writers from other nations and visited the grave of one of her acknowledged heroes, Paul Valéry. They spent a year in the United States in 1979 and 1980, during which time Berenguer presented her work at numerous colleges and universities. Oddly, some overviews of her literary generation have asserted Berenguer's importance, yet—in a curious double move—also limited remarks on Berenguer to little more than a mention of her marriage to Díaz, a radical foreshortening of her activities.

Beyond generating an impressive list of books that alone demonstrates her significance, Berenguer maintained a strong presence in magazines in her region, gained increasing recognition abroad, assumed leadership of cultural programs in Montevideo, and generally dedicated time to her fellow writers. In the 1960s, when the famous critic Ángel Rama led the literary section of *Marcha*, the Southern Cone's leading left-wing newspaper, she frequently figured in its pages. At the end of that decade, Berenguer became part of a writers' circle associated with the French intellectuals Paul Fleury and Lucien Mercer, who came to Montevideo and founded the French/Uruguayan magazine *Maldoror* (a reference to Ducasse).

By the 1970s Berenguer was receiving more international recognition. A striking event highlighted by her Uruguayan editors came in 1970, after her poem "Primera conjugación" had appeared in the Havana magazine *Casa de las Américas*: Cuban dance superstar Alicia Alonso performed a piece entitled "Conjugación," based on Berenguer's poem, with the island's National Ballet. In 1977 Berenguer began a three-year period directing the *Pliegos de Arte y Poesía* (Art and Poetry Pages) project with the Radio Sarandí Book Club, followed by work with this same group on volumes dedicated to her great Uruguayan predecessor Delmira Agustini (1886-1914). Another activity illustrating her awareness of poetry as an art form moving beyond the page was Berenguer's 1982 collaboration with other prominent writers and musicians in an event dedicated to performances of poetry, prose, and music. For this event, she worked with another one of Uruguay's poetry greats, Marosa di Giorgio, as well as the experimental composer Juan José Iturriberry.

The winner of various prizes and other recognitions for her own poetry, Berenguer was invited to serve as a juror in many competitions, such as the prestigious Casa de las Américas Prize for Poetry for 1986. During her lifetime she also received invitations to present her work in a variety of nations—Berenguer was often the sole Uruguayan, or one of very few, invited to *encuentros* (gatherings or conferences) featuring poets from Latin America and abroad—and she saw her poetry translated into French and German, with a limited number of pieces also appearing in English.

Lively, sonorous, constantly exploring new realms, her complete collections are brilliantly conceived and powerful, but they have yet to be fully appreciated by English-language readers. Given Berenguer's immense talent and prolific publication record, it is surprising that her work was not translated into English more extensively before now. Some individual poems have been translated into English for scattered anthologies and a few prominent journals since the 1980s (such as the Americas Society's New York-based *Review*, historically essential in promoting the translation of Latin American literature in the United States, and *American Poetry Review*, as well as *Tamaqua*). These include renditions by Louise Popkin, Deborah Bonner, and Margaret Sayers Peden. Some translations into English were probably encouraged by Berenguer's extended visit to the United States in 1979–1980. Another prompt was her participation in a 1986 symposium at the University of Maryland, which focused on extreme repression and the reconstruction of culture in Uruguay. For this occasion, Popkin translated a poem that Berenguer had composed a few months earlier. "The Signs on the Table"/"Los signos sobre la mesa" opens with a devastating question: "What metaphor could possibly convey / the headless slaughtered thunderclap of pain / and lay the signs on the table?" [2]

---

2   In *Repression, Exile, and Democracy: Uruguayan Culture*. Eds. Saúl Sosnowski and Louise B. Popkin. Tr. Louise B. Popkin. Durham: Duke UP, 1993. 162-177.

Two more recent anthologies of Uruguayan literature in English translation now include excerpts of strong work by Berenguer that can help readers to appreciate more of her span. These are *Contemporary Uruguayan Poetry: A Bilingual Anthology* (Bucknell UP, 2010; edited by Ronald Haladyna) and *Hotel Lautréamont: Contemporary Poetry from Uruguay* (Shearsman Books, 2011; edited by Kent Johnson and Roberto Echavarren). But anyone can see that it takes a full-length selection dedicated to Amanda Berenguer for English-language readers to comprehend her tremendous, multidirectional writing career and overall significance in Latin American letters. (Readers of Spanish may also wish to consult the major critical anthology of Amir Hamed, *Orientales: Uruguay a través de su poesía* [Siglo XX, 1996], in which Berenguer's work is extensively discussed and identified as one of the nation's major literary achievements of the twentieth century.) Jesse Lee Kercheval has organized a series of recent and ongoing projects focused on women writers from Uruguay, and she is at work on a future Southern Cone anthology. She included poems by Berenguer in translation in a 2017 magazine feature for *Western Humanities Review*. The Library of Congress recently posted audio recordings of Berenguer at their website, a welcome addition.

Finally, we're pleased to include supplementary material showcasing questions and observations about her work from two other renowned contemporary Uruguayan poets, Roberto Echavarren and Silvia Guerra. Echavarren, Berenguer's literary co-executor, offers reflections drawn from his long and intimate knowledge of her poetry, while Guerra conducted a poignant interview with Berenguer not long before the poet's death, which Jeannine Marie Pitas has now delivered in an English translation.

Note on the Translations

The recreation of Berenguer's poems in English is a complex process. Poetry translators inevitably see two—or many more—ways to render passages. Sometimes our translators selected a translation that is not perfectly literal, in terms of dictionary definition, in order to capture another quality of the poem.

One twist involves reactivating literal reference to the Spanish when the source word or phrase is not part of more common usage in the target language. For example, Jeannine Marie Pitas remarks that the most common English translation of the *Palo de agua* plant appearing in "The Plants and the Radio" is "Cornstalk Dracaena." Instead she created the name "Water Cornstalk" with Berenguer's poem as a whole in mind. Pitas' choice makes direct reference to water, evoking the *agua* of the plant's name in Spanish.

The translations of Berenguer's visual poems from the early 1970s add intricacy to the usual debates about how to balance competing priorities in poetry translation. Graphic elements of her presentation not only make translation more difficult but multiply the potential strategies available to the translator. We asked Urayoán Noel how he would like to approach this material. An accomplished bilingual poet and scholar, Noel decided to push his translation toward free interpretations of each poem, prioritizing Berenguer's overall creative play with words and graphics.

Some details of Berenguer's poetry vary amongst editions printed in Spanish. Most material in this bilingual edition follows the 2002 anthology, *Constelación del navío (Poesía 1950-2002)*. The originals of the "Arena" visual sequence are scanned here from *Arena* (Centro de Artes y Letras de Punta del Este, 1978); we followed Roberto Echavarren's recommendation to use a title with each segment, a decision made for Berenguer's 2002 anthology. Anna Deeny Morales consulted the 1983 Arca edition of *Identidad de ciertas frutas*. Kristin Dykstra used the 1987 edition of *La dama de Elche* in dialogue with the later anthology. Dykstra and Johnson based the poems from *La cuidadora del fuego* on the 2010 edition from Uruguayan publisher La Flauta Mágica, the same book where the interview translated by Pitas appeared in Spanish.

Amanda Berenguer: Some Notes by Way of Preface
Roberto Echavarren

Three years ago, Amanda Berenguer told me she had a book ready. Its title would be *La cuidadora del fuego* (*The Keeper of the Flame*). Could I write the prologue? "Fine," I said, "where is the book?" She pointed to a pile of notebooks, seven in total, fattened by loose papers, notes, bills. On the reverse of a check she had scribbled a short poem: "Final." Such notebooks were Amanda's *vademecum*. Everything was thrown together in them, her poems mixed with notations about household affairs.

Amanda had no computer and no typewriter. "You should get someone to sort out the poems and type them for you," I would say in one fashion or another, now and again. Soon she became too ill to make any arrangements about that. By Amanda's birthday in 2009, she was no longer able to work on the poems. I suggested to Dr. Álvaro Díaz Berenguer, her son and executor, that I compile *La cuidadora del fuego* from her notebooks, and he agreed.

Transcribing the verses, I maintained the horizontal *tiret* she used to divide one segment of the verse from another, in a way reminiscent of Emily Dickinson. Amanda had translated several of Dickinson's poems. This suspension, this dash, creates a pause, both in order to ponder what has been said and to prepare for what follows. Thought advances by steps, and the reader should take her time also, in order to appreciate and relish what is being offered. Amanda's poetry is an exercise of the intelligence, a testing of perception, an examination of spatial conundrums such as the Möbius strip or Klein bottle, figures explicitly investigated by Berenguer in books like *Materia prima* (*Prime Matter*) and *La botella verde* (*The Green Bottle*). Topology is a geometrical discipline linked to mathematics which studies the engendering of some forms out of others. A rectangle elongates and folds on itself, in two faces that are also one: the Möbius strip; a surface curves and invaginates itself: a Klein bottle. Intuition, here, is not the negation of reason but a faculty that questions it from the perspective of lived experience. Insight and vision have to do with life, with movement and change, with mutable qualities and difference, rather than with quantity or unity.

The book that brought her to immediate critical attention, both in Uruguay and beyond, is *Materia Prima* (1966), which includes one of her most famous poems, "Las nubes magallánicas" ("The Magellanic Clouds"). For Amanda, the incorporeal is nothing but the body's capacity for segregating indefinitely modulated, puzzling shapes through movement. The soul is a movable feast born with the body. The soul is the modifier of space.

One could say that Amanda's poetics is supported by physics. Following this view, a poet most akin to her would be Lucretius. Amanda herself was stimulated by Leonardo da Vinci's inventions of space. "Las nubes magallánicas" is an astronomical poem witnessing the procession of the galaxies from a female body stretched on the rocks by the coast: Andromeda exposed, both on earth (the poet) and in the sky (a galaxy of the same name).

Andromeda's body on the rock. The soul inventing spatial sky, an invention of forms emerging from forms, a process, an associated unfolding of their various streams. Everything manifests here and also there: the scientific account of physical processes drives a poetic impulse when reference is obliterated by the sheer suggestive relevance of the words themselves—effects, echoes—that which exceeds information.

A flight through the galaxies starts from a female body, poised on the rocks. The flight of the soul, and the physiology of the body. Nothing is left out of the poem, although everything is stylized. "Las nubes magallánicas" can be compared to "El sueño" ("The Dream"), the canonical seventeenth century poem by Juana Inés de la Cruz. They both bring a nocturnal experience to light, the constelled sky. The sky as the place of thought and elations of the spirit, of elucubration and conjecture, the body as realm, supporter, the working physiological condition for experience and achievement. Everything is implicated—the soul and the body, outside and inside, like the two surfaces of the Möbius strip which are one. Everything takes place in time: is that time linear or circular? It seems clear that she explores both modes.

La cuidadora del fuego is her last book; a calm, nearly classical summation of her work. The view from her study, the birds and plants in her yard, changes of light, the inception of the seasons. In this scenic parterre, all her resources for emotional felicity are present, not least a keen awareness of the encroachment of death.

Each poem by Amanda questions our reason from a specific angle: "La dama de Elche" ("The Lady of Elche"), "Los culos de El Bosco" ("The Asses of Bosch"). Poetry (in her) is a powerful intelligence, the novelty of astonishment and delight.

June 2012, Montevideo

Books by Amanda Berenguer

A través de los tiempos que llevan a la gran calma (1940)

Canto hermético (1941)

Elegía por la muerte de Paul Valéry (1945)

El río (1952)

Suficiente maravilla (1953-1954)

La invitación (1957)

Contracanto (1961)

Quehaceres e invenciones (1963)

Declaración conjunta (1964)

Materia prima (1966)

Dicciones (1973) [audio]

Composición de lugar (1976)

Arena (1978)

El tigre alfabetario (1979)

Poesía [1949–1979] (1980)

Identidad de ciertas frutas (1983)

La dama de Elche (1987)

Los signos sobre la mesa (1987)

La botella verde (Analysis situs) (1995)

El pescador de caña (1995)

La estranguladora (1998)

Escritos (2000)

Poner la mesa del tercer milenio (2002)

Constelación del navío [a selected anthology] (2002)

La cuidadora del fuego (2010)

Additional shorter publications include:

El monstruo incesante. Expedición de caza (1990)

Las mil y una preguntas y propicios contextos (2005)

Casas donde viven criaturas del lenguaje y el diccionario (2005)

Poems

de *Materia Prima*

from **Prime Matter** (1966)

translated by Mónica de la Torre

Objeto volador no identificado

Viene directamente de huevo desciende
de anillo surge de aviso
brota de viaducto tiembla de intacto
salta de vivero en vivero anda
de cuerpo planta como mueble mar
o árbol radio semejante
a un capitel de piedra filosofal
a nervio centro a hueso eje
parece un arma en sí
útil concreto
intento fuerza
humor fénix
o cosa enardecida además
nube negra horadante
viaje al fin de la noche
ave gas robot futuro anterior
libro de bitácora incendiado
alado Leonardo renaciente
Paracelso subiendo
en un pueblo mercurial
viejo Picasso radioactivo magnético
órgano electrónico artilugio
saltimbanqui afuera azar Odisea
botella al mar
vamos de prisa explotaremos
nos daremos de cara contra el sueño
pasaremos oh sí región Einstein
rayos y centellas

OBJETO discoidal platiforme despliegue
máquina rutilante a 45 grados
sobre el horizonte noria
virando de sur a norte
rueda intermitente trompoviento

Unidentified Flying Object

Comes directly from egg descends
from ring arises from warning
springs from overpass trembles intact
leaps from nursery to nursery goes around
like a body plant like furniture sea
or tree radius similar
to a philosopher's stone capital
to central nerve to bone axis
resembles a weapon itself
useful concrete
attempt force
phoenix mood
or thing ablaze also
burrowing black cloud
journey to the end of the night
bird gas robot prior future
logbook on fire
winged Leonardo renascent
Paracelsus ascending
in a mercurial town
old Picasso radioactive magnetic
electronic organ gizmo
acrobat outside chance Odyssey
bottle out to sea
we rush we will explode
we will crash against sleep head on
we will go through oh yes Einstein region
thunderbolts

UN— formerly difficult impossible void
alone in the desert senseless
absentminded orphaned left
mute and blind nobody
to stay vegetate linger
it is worthless unimportant useless

nave celular en los tejidos celestes
artificio mecánico probable
circuito abierto
descansemos
observemos la terrible realidad
naranja propulsora a la vista emitiendo

VOLADOR alígero alieter alisonda alingenio
vértigo atento espacial salvoconducto
la velocidad es una trampa
de la memoria
los cambios de rumbo
una celada del tiempo
movamos los telescopios y adelante
con los pozos y las bolsas de carbón
de la galaxia

NO antes difícil imposible vacío
en el desierto a solas sin sentido
desmemoriado huérfano dejado
mudo y ciego nadie
quedarse vegetar durar
no vale no importa no sirve para nada

IDENTIFICADO signo de algo tabulado
hay instrucciones precisas
para su captura
estamos en el secreto compartido
nombrado
válgame hombre qué poderes
la materia apalabrada
imaginada
certifico ver lo que vemos
lo soñado contigo presente
para atestiguar lo incierto

IDENTIFIED sign of something tabulated
there are precise instructions
for its capture
we dwell in the shared secret
named
oh man what powers
matter put into words
imagined
I certify I see what we see
what I dreamt of with you present
to witness the uncertain

FLYING winged wingether wingprobe wingenious
attentive vertigo spatial go-ahead
speed is the trap
of memory
the changes of direction
time's ambush
let us move the telescopes and go forward
with the galaxy's
wells and coalsacks

OBJECT discus-like plate-shaped display
sparkling machine at 45 degrees
over the horizon treadmill
turning from south to north
intermittent wheel windspin
cellular spacecraft in the celestial tissues
mechanical artifice probable
open circuit
let us rest
let us contemplate the terrible reality
orange engine in sight emitting

UFO manifest visible discovered
glorious

OVNI aflorado visible descubierto
glorioso
casi flor casi animal
casi aparato interior casi certeza
casi la trasmutación de la materia
espiritual como un gato
al calor infrarrojo del sueño
suburbano como el coraje
anotado en una pantalla de radar
refractario como la cara del amor
cuando tiene la mirada
en otra parte
denso como una idea salida de madre
discontinuo como el placer
radiante como un cromosoma
en cielo tinto portaobjeto
portaestandarte
con una sigla en onda corta
portaequipaje portaespecie

vamos detrás formando cola
con un niño de la mano
un pequeño cohete teleguiado
bajo el brazo
dos o tres revistas de historietas
en la valija
un aparato portátil de televisión
una lata de carne conservada
y un frasco de dulce de duraznos
yo puedo llevar aún una maceta
con un filodendro enano
o algo que no se llame rosal
pero que dé rosas de otro nombre
igual a las rosas de verdad
y un deseo salvaje aclimatado
unido al soporte

almost flower almost animal
almost interior device almost certainty
almost transmutation of spiritual
matter like a cat
exposed to the infrared heat of the suburban
dream like anger
annotated on a radar screen
heat-resistant like love's face
when its gaze
is elsewhere
dense like an idea sprung from mother
discontinuous like pleasure
radiant like a chromosome
in a microscope slide sky-red portfire
standard bearer
with an acronym on shortwave
portmanteau portfolio

we stand behind forming a line
holding a child by the hand
a small rocket teleguided
under our arms
two or three comic books
in our suitcase
a portable television
canned meat
and a jar of peach marmalade
I can even bring a potted
dwarf philodendron
or something not called a rosebush
that produces roses with another name
identical to real roses
and a wild desire acclimated
united to the support
of the indispensable parachute
the family ready gathered

del imprescindible paracaídas
la familia pronta reunida
en un círculo continuo
vertiginoso tú el padre
y tú el hijo y tú la madre
las hélices los tubos los chorros
de vida cotidiana salpicando
la atmósfera
listos para el vuelo
entremos a la cámara blindada
montemos ese dromedario centrífugo
sigamos la mirada hacia el génesis
de Mona Lisa
su órbita de cilias urticantes
despeguemos desde la base colgante
la intermediaria luna ocasional
ahora tan a mano

palpo lentamente
una cinta de Moebius siento
ese breve vértigo de entrecasa
o escalofrío en su jaula
toco ese pájaro por fuera
y esa ostra por dentro sucesivos
palpitantes
su unilátera hoja ambigua
hermafrodita
exterior e interior a un mismo tiempo
lo que no sabemos
resbala bajo los dedos
cae en un barril sin fondo

desaparece a ojos vistas
se pierde en el fragor de la batalla
sacando chispas insultos gritos
reto a las tinieblas

in an unbroken circle
vertiginous you the father
and you the child and you the mother
the propellers the tubes the jets
of everyday life spraying
the atmosphere
ready for flight
let us enter the armored chamber
let us mount that centrifugal dromedary
let us turn our eyes toward the genesis
of Mona Lisa
its orbit of stinging cilia
let us take off from the hanging base
the intermediary occasional moon
so within reach now

I slowly sense
a Möbius strip I feel
that brief vertigo of homeliness
or a shudder in its cage
I touch that bird on the outside
and oyster on the inside successive
palpitating
its unilateral ambiguous leaf
hermaphrodite
exterior and interior at once
the unknown
drips down our fingers
falls into a bottomless well

visibly disappears
loses itself in the battle's uproar
spewing sparks insults screams
challenges the darkness
the gauntlet thrown down
look there it goes

quedó arrojado el guante
míralo allá va
la mano abierta ingrávida
con una gota de sangre coagulada
en su anular vacío
palpando la azarosa orquídea
de espacio foliado intermitente
alfabeto Morse a pétalos cifrados
el gesto suspenso a la deriva
tanteando la puerta del mundo
mientras dura una pausa
del pensamiento
brilla la amnesia expuesta punzante
desconocida vía Láctea.

the weightless open hand
with a drop of congealed blood
on its empty ring finger
feeling the random orchid
of intermittent foliated space
Morse alphabet of ciphered petals
the gesture suspended adrift
taking measure of the world's door
in the lapse
of thought's pause
the exposed piercing amnesia shines
the Milky Way unknown.

La cinta de Moebius

Palpo lentamente
una cinta de Moebius siento
ese breve vértigo de entrecasa
o escalofrío en su jaula toco
ese pájaro por fuera y esa ostra por dentro
sucesivos palpitantes
sigo su unilátera hoja ambigua
hermafrodita
exterior e interior a un mismo tiempo

pulso el insalubre vibrátil sedimento
de la pura verdad
los seudópodos hacia lo oscuro
las ideas de paso sonámbulo que andan
por los alrededores de las doce del día
la celda callada la pieza "se alquila"
en el patio de la ruidosa boca ciudadana

rozo marchitas flores de visión
recién polinizadas
sus hojas de foca brillante a cuenta
de negra primavera los cuerpos de pelo lacio
de fibra córnea escamosa colgados
en los andenes ahumados o en los muelles
donde los changadores escupen tierra
o en los salones para pasajeros

así resortes trabados en cajas fuertes
recuerdos
así bengalas sin encender
recuerdos
así expresos estacionados vacíos
recuerdos acaricio
la memoria pronta a saltar elástica

Möbius Strip

I slowly sense
a Möbius strip feel
that brief vertigo of homeliness
or a shudder in its cage I touch
that bird on the outside and oyster on the inside
successive palpitating
I follow its unilateral ambiguous leaf
hermaphrodite
exterior and interior at once

I press the noxious vibrating sediment
of pure truth
the pseudopods reaching toward the dark
the sleepwalking ideas pacing
about around noon
the quiet cell the room "for rent"
in the patio of the loud citizen mouth

I brush against wilting flowers of vision
recently pollinated
their shiny seal leaves on account
of a black spring the straight-haired bodies
of scaly cornea fiber hanging
on the smoky platforms or the docks
where the porters spit dirt
or in the passenger lounges

hence springs jammed in safes
memories
hence unused sparklers
memories
hence parked express trains empty
memories I caress
the memory ready to jump elastic

una fotografía instantánea sobre el pretil
de la oficina de treinta pisos fábrica
en Tokio o Brasilia
hacia la posición natural de descanso

tanteo recorro camino la otra cara
la fabulosa cara la doble cara la misma
cara tu cara anacrónica
mi cara alquimia social
¿te asustas? ¿respiras? ¿comprendes?
te veo y nos ven sobremanera
el rostro semblante fachada
o superficie anterior no olvides
recuerda el anverso presencia
marchando a hasta para por
según sin sobre tras la cara de dos vueltas
interminables

apura cara de juez tu veredicto
escucha cara del montón escucha
cara de perro otra y otra más
cara de pocos amigos no mezcles
grasa aceite agua hirviendo
cara de vinagre
cara de risa la expresa
que viste y calza máscara para gases
cara y cruz abrazadas
gestando huevos de oro en la bodega
de la "Santa María" hollando el Aqueronte
dispara carabina ametralladora
hasta el caracú profundo caracú expuesto
¡caramba! carantamaula
resbalo entro cavo
esta cueva centrípeta refugio
atrayente mina carbonífera
(32 mil metros cúbicos de roca viva

an instant photo on the parapet
of a thirty-story office building a factory
in Tokyo or Brasilia
toward the natural resting position

I probe traverse walk on the other face
the fabulous face the double face the same
face your anachronistic face
my face social alchemy
scared? are you breathing? get it?
I see you and they see us exceedingly
a face countenance façade
or prior surface do not forget
remember the front side presence
marching toward until in order to because of
as per without over behind the face of two interminable
turns

hurry judge-face your verdict
listen face-in-the-crowd listen
dog-face and yet another one
long-face don't mix
grease oil boiling water
vinegar-face
funny-face the manifest
none other than the one with a gas mask
heads and tails embracing
producing golden eggs in the cellar
of the "Santa María" crossing the Acheron
fire rifle sub-machine gun
reach the deep marrow the exposed marrow
holy smokes! hideous mask
I slide I enter I dig
this centripetal cave shelter
alluring carboniferous mine
(32 thousand cubic meters of live rock

para abrir el túnel del Simplón)
atestada de diamantes venenosos
canjeables por vida por menos
que vida por vida desvivida
este corredor sin salida corredor
en derredor ovillo alrededor del lazo enroscado
escalera rampa encaracolada
¿quién de nosotros quién
le encuentra el cabo a madeja?
vagabundos caminantes ahí
ahí en el hueco de tu mano

se ven ahí
las tres inciertas parcas mineras
investigadoras educando
conejos de India filamentos eléctricos
murciélagos de onda ultra corta
para un curso experimental
de expertos en corruptología
ahí en el fondo en la cripta anunciación
subimos paloma uterina escudo
caparazón cúpula de barro arriba ascensor
muro Le Corbusier cielo de cemento
último piso
torre esferoidal de acero construcción
voladiza en ladrillos de vidrio
techo astronómico boquiabierto
astrolabio
provisto de limbos graduados
para medir el ángulo sujeto a error
de la eternidad entre nosotros
entre casa observatorio
entre tú y yo amantes
hechos una misma velocidad de cuerpo y alma
alunizamos en nuestro propio corazón
dimos la vuelta a la tierra de Moebius
marchamos sobre su pista enguantada
a kilómetros años luz de vertiginosa
felicidad

to build the Simplon Tunnel)
rife with poisonous diamonds
redeemable for life for less
than life for the liveliest life
this corridor with no exit looping
corridor ball of yarn around the coiled rope
winding staircase ramp
which of us finds the skein's end?
vagabonds wanderers there
there in the hollow of your hand

you see there
the three uncertain Fates miners
researchers educating
Guinea pigs electric filaments
bats of ultra short wave
for an experimental course
taught by experts on corruptology
there at the end of the annunciation crypt
we ascend uterine dove shield
shell clay cupola elevator up
Le Corbusier wall cement sky
top floor
spherical steel tower cantilevered
construction of glass bricks
astronomical ceiling openmouthed
astrolabe
equipped with limbs calibrated
to measure the angle subject to error
of the eternity between us
between the observatory house
between you and I lovers
turned into a same body-and-soul velocity
we moonland on own heart
we circled Möbius's earth
we marched over its gloved field
at kilometers light years from vertiginous
bliss

Las Nubes Magallánicas

cuando transitamos a velocidad cotidiana
la gran avenida vía Láctea paseo
cielo parque conocido desde niña y
antes aún de papá y mamá muy semejante
a 18 de julio cuando mirábamos pasar
desde el chevrolet 36 detenido en la acera
las personas preparadas para una exposición
rodante con aire de retreta y repasaba
un examen de historia natural
y sus vidrieras falsas de vida nocturna amarillenta
en bajo voltaje sobrecargado a punto de estallar
y se enciende el motor y se cruzan las calles
de la Aguada la estación de tranvías del Reducto
con reloj en hora hasta el Brazo Oriental
de vuelta por San Martín entre plátanos jóvenes
hasta Huáscar corta y sin hormigonar y cuando

llegamos a casa ahora en otro lado
del mapa de la ciudad en la punta
más cerca de un labio del planeta
cuando volvemos a esta turbia clara
circunvalación suburbana
mezclados de yema central y del ruido
usurero de un río de plata baja
batiendo contra el murallón de la rambla
costanera o crecido sobre la orilla arenosa
apretando un huevo puesto en pleno vuelo
así con la cáscara partida Montevideo derramado
por un pájaro parecido al ave tiempo
del segundo viaje de Simbad
y cuando es hora de amor y de ladrones
en el monte de al lado
o cuando sobre la playa me tiro al agua
entre los crustáceos al fondo en su elemento

The Magellanic Clouds

when we travel at everyday speed
across the great avenue Milky Way a promenade
sky park known since childhood and
even before mother and father very similar
to Avenue 18 de julio when we would see go by
from a '36 chevy stopped by the side of the road
people prepared for a traveling
exhibition redolent of carnival and I'd go over
a natural history examination
and its fake showcases of yellowish night life
in low voltage overloaded to the point of near explosion
and the engine's turned on and we drive through the streets
of the Aguada neighborhood and the tram station of Reducto
with the clock on the dot until reaching the Brazo Oriental
returning through San Martin amid young plane trees
arriving at the short unpaved street of Huáscar and when

we arrive home now in a different location
on the city's map on the tip
closest to one of the planet's lips
when we return to this muddy clear
suburban loop
mixed with the central yolk and the greedy
noise of a river low in silver
lashing the coastal rambla's seawall
or rising over its sandy edge
squeezing an egg lain during flight
there it is with its cracked shell Montevideo spilled
by a bird akin to the bird of time
in Sinbad's second voyage
and when it is time for lovers and thieves
on the nearby hill
or when at the beach I jump in the water
amid the crustaceans at the bottom in their element

o a un pozo para desaparecer o morir
de otra envergadura en otro viaje
navegando surcando el agua negra
a la pesca de presas de oro prometidas
abierto hasta los tuétanos el tesoro
de los antepasados latinos industriosos y avaros

quedan someras sobras sobre la mesa tendida
queso para trampas caseras y cebo rancio
y lentejas con tocino guisadas
para alimentar los diarios malos entendidos
viejos como el mundo
un plato por otro de carne viva fría
o trozos dando coletazos de eso que somos
por dentro y no se ve
y emerge a veces en rabiosa pesca mayor
difícil de descuartizar

aventamos las plumas indemnes sepultadas
de aves americanas o de indios charrúas
entusiastas asadores de Solís el descubridor
de este lecho correntoso donde aún desovan
las corvinas con cangrejilla y los delfines maman
sin línea directa a ningún trono de la tierra
y se enturbia una resaca misionera colonial

cuando ocurre un accidente
y muere un niño ciclista aplastado
contra el parabrisas asesino del automóvil
en Caramurú junto al arroyo
cuando suena el despertador y repica el pulso
en las coronarias
cuando me despierto y recuerdo

alguien está mirando directamente nuestra espalda
el codo pelado la nuca las vértebras lumbares

or into a well to disappear or die
with a different breadth in another voyage
navigating crossing the black water
fishing for the promised prey of gold
opened to its marrow the treasure
of our Latin ancestors industrious and miserly

there are scant leftovers on the set table
cheese for homemade traps and rancid fodder
and lentils cooked with bacon
to feed the daily misunderstandings
as old as the world
one dish for another of cold live flesh
or thrashing pieces of what we are
inside and is invisible
and sometimes emerges in a raging major catch
difficult to dismember

we toss out the buried unscathed feathers
of American birds or of Charrúa Indians
enthusiastic stabbers of Solís the discoverer
of the bed of this rapid stream where even
baited corvina fish spawn and dolphins suck milk
without a direct line to any of the world's thrones
and a missionary colonial undertow muddies

when an accident happens
and a boy on his bike dies crushed
against the murderous windshield of a car
in Caramurú near a stream
when the alarm clock goes off and the pulse drums
in the coronary arteries
when I wake up and remember

someone is staring directly at our backs
our bare elbows our napes our lumbar vertebrae

que sólo conocemos por dentro
en el interior del espejo en la penumbra
de una radiografía
o el repliegue astuto de la oreja palpable
o la cara oculta de la luna observando
con una lupa de tiempo
ampliando el espectro en sus fantasmas
verdaderos

las Nubes de Magallanes encienden en los alrededores de
nuestro polo celeste austral dos jirones arrancados a la
vía Láctea de forma vagamente circular
la Gran Nube se extiende en la constelación de la Dorada
la Pequeña Nube en la constelación del Tucán
la Gran Nube contiene estrellas supergigantes azules o
rojas nebulosas gaseosas de emisión por ejemplo una de
las más luminosas del firmamento la nebulosa de la
Tarántula y cefeidas típicas y polvos absorbentes que no
dejan ver las galaxias alejadas la Pequeña Nube en
cambio es transparente

se descubren puentes de materia retorcidos formando bucles desplegados a
semejanza de tenues ramajes o estirados al máximo y casi quebrados existe
un fondo luminoso continuo en las regiones centrales de los grandes cúmulos
de galaxias la difusión es uniforme y granada más o menos quinientos millones
por ahora de gérmenes de infinito ah! entrego parte de un botín de guerra
diaria en prenda por un largo corredor o paso de materia recién descubierto

el mar es cada vez más liviano y hondo
la respiración suave acompasada
el pensamiento apenas esbozado
por palabras sencillas
el cielo abierto de pie sostiene a pulso
nuestras preguntas de rigor

which we only know from within
from the inside of a mirror in the half-light
of an x-ray
or the astute crease of our palpable ear
or the dark side of the moon contemplating
with a magnifying glass of time
amplifying the spectrum with its true
ghosts

the Magellanic Clouds light in the surroundings
of our austral celestial pole two wisps torn from the
Milky Way their shape is vaguely circular
the Large Cloud extends to the constellation of Dorado
the Small Cloud to the constellation of Tucana
the Large Cloud contains supergiant stars either blue
or red emission nebulae for instance one of the
firmament's most luminous the Tarantula Nebula
and Classical Cepheids and absorbent dust blocking
distant galaxies from view the Small Cloud on the
contrary is see-through

one discovers bridges of twisted matter forming curls either unfurled and
resembling tenuous branches or stretched to the limit and almost broken there
is a continuous luminous backdrop in the central regions of the great clusters
of galaxies diffusion is uniform and judicious more or less five hundred
million embryos for now of infinitude ah! I turn in part of a daily war booty
as pledge through a long corridor or a recently discovered pathway of matter

the sea is ever lighter and deeper
breath soft and rhythmic
thought barely outlined
by simple words
the upright open sky painstakingly sustains
our de rigueur questions

el viejo por qué deforme
con sus débiles huesos contrahechos

el plano galáxico se halla cubierto por nubes de gas
polvoriento alineadas a lo largo de las espiras

la imagen más simple y correcta del universo es
todavía la de un espacio euclidiano regularmente
poblado de este animal enloquecido mordiéndose la
cola y pariendo estrellas que miramos cada noche
sin ver en la oscuridad más allá de nuestros ojos

el sur y el norte prevalecen luchando en un circo cerrado
se da vuelta el hemisferio austral donde nacimos
abrimos con el navegante Magallanes y los sesenta bramadores
su estrecho pasaje y giramos al norte
de un solo espacio todopoderoso
estaba cercano entonces del otro lado infinito
la incorruptible mujer encadenada a poca distancia
del polo boreal
la gran espiral Messier 31 de Andrómeda
expuesta hasta los ovarios destellantes
entre los tejidos borbotando sombra
atada a una roca radioactiva radiofuente
radioeléctrica
a la orilla de un océano de frías olas de hidrógeno
cayendo sobre sus flancos de virgo devota Persea
nebulosa foca o vaca marina entre los árabes
también encadenada

zumba el ruido de fondo de la galaxia
una sierra sin fin preparando el árbol del silencio
en muestras micrométricas
canta la marea boscosa del tremendo mar
este mismo mar sucio de arrastre o río grande
como mar Paraná Guazú salado y dulce

why the old man deformed
his weak bones misshapen

the galactic plane is covered by clouds of dusty
gas along the spires

the simplest and most accurate image of the universe is
still that of an Euclidean space regularly
inhabited by this deranged animal biting its
tail and spawning stars that we see every night
without seeing anything in the dark beyond our eyes

south and north continue wrestling in a closed circus
the austral hemisphere where we were born turns
we open with seafarer Magellan and the sixty bellowers
his narrow strait and then we veer north
of a sole almighty space
the other infinite space was then nearby
the incorruptible chained woman in close proximity
to the boreal pole
Andromeda's great spiral Messier 31
exposed even her dazzling ovaries
between tissues gurgling shadows
she tied to a radioactive radiofountain
radioelectric rock
on the edge of an ocean of cold hydrogen waves
breaking on her flanks of devout virgo Persea
nebulous seal or marine cow among the Arabs
also chained

the buzz of the galaxy's background noise
a saw endlessly preparing the tree of silence
in micrometrical samples
the forested tide sings of a tremendous ocean
this very ocean dirtied by the pull or a river as big
as an ocean Paraná Guazú with saltwater and fresh water

en el entrevero y una mujer desnuda sobre las rocas
entre playa Verde y playa Honda con los pies
donde golpean las olas esperando al amante que traerá
de los correosos pelos la cabeza de Medusa junto
al juego de anillos como regalo de bodas
golpean rompen las olas de hidrógeno sobre los flancos
desnudos sobre la gran espiral
Messier 31 de Andrómeda sobre esa mujer
asoleándose
extendiéndose caliente y tersa
con los brazos firmes en la axila y el cuerpo de
pan bien amasado pronto para el horno de una playa desierta
los redondos senos contra el sol mostrando
las palpitantes cefeidas y el sexo de humo espeso
respirando a empujones sobre esa mujer sola
asoleándose sobre Andrómeda en puro cuerpo
sobre la gran espiral Messier 31 encadenada a la espera
estaba una noche en las rocas de la plaza Virgilio
vigilando el Río de la Plata atenta
al contrabando de las aguas por el mismo cielo
a través de un ojo de bronce
abierto a los caídos en el mar
aguardaba el tránsito suntuoso de la nave Argos
a toda luz en la altura desplegada cerca del sur celeste
hundida la quilla en la negra onda hasta Canope
el piloto alfa de la Carena a la vista siempre
en su encrespada línea de flotación
no tenía apuro y no podía moverme
la espalda entumida al contacto de la dura oscuridad
apenas arribaba a la costa un ruido periódico
volcando una redada de segundos
recién pescados y todavía vivos

cuando se está solo se sienten más
fuertes las ligaduras y el peso real
del leve firmamento extendido
sobre el cuerpo afiebrado

in the mêlée and a woman lying naked on the rocks
between Playa Verde and Playa Honda her feet
where the waves break waiting for the lover lugging
Medusa's head by its coarse hair along with
a set of rings as a wedding gift
the hydrogen waves crash and break on the bare
flanks on the great spiral
Andromeda's Messier 31 above the sunbathing
woman
splayed warm and soft
with arms firm on her armpits and a body of
well-kneaded bread ready for the oven of a desert beach
her round breasts facing the sun showing
the palpitating Cepheids and the thick smoky sex
breathing heavily over the lone woman
her full body sunbathing over Andromeda
on the great spiral Messier 31 chained waiting
one night she was on the rocks of Plaza Virgilio
keeping vigil over the Río de la Plata attentive to
the very sky's smuggling of water
with her eye of bronze
open to the sea's fallen
I awaited the sumptuous transit of the Argo
visibly traversing the heights near the celestial south
the keel plunging in the black wave toward Canopus
the alpha pilot of Carina always in view
in its broken up waterline
I was in no rush and I could not move
my back numb upon contact with the stiff darkness
an intermittent noise faintly heard on the coast
turning over a raid of newly fished
and still live seconds

when one is alone the ligatures and real heft
of the lightweight firmament extended
over the feverish body
are felt more intensely

el Navío se acercaba lentamente balanceando
su popa y volviendo al puerto de partida

no podía saber cuál era su destino
no creo que pasara por allí
por el sitio aquel donde esperaba
¿acaso el propio Argos podría
descubrir el escondrijo situado
en una punta montevideana
donde permanezco atada a esta escritura?

las estrellas se detienen posadas en el mástil
y aletean sacudiendo el profundo duermevela
la noche es larga y todo pasa cerca
y sigue trajinando
en la pulsación se mide la distancia
se sabe la temida trayectoria se numeran
los latidos que nos restan de la suma inicial
entregada a cuenta del propio corazón
¿Andrómeda eres tú aquella insomne nebulosa o
ésta que soy ahora transitoria aquí en la tierra?
pasa el Navío enarbolado en toda su gloria
sobre el meridiano
recuerda: el viejo Ptolomeo catalogó en la constelación cuarenta y cinco
estrellas en orden similar al de un tratado sobre la forma de construir barcos
los astrónomos modernos la dividen y le detallan quilla popa mástil vela pero
sólo la mitad trasera del buque asoma a la carta de navegación de altura
andando de tal suerte en su carrera nocturna de este a oeste que la popa va
delante retrocediendo en la dirección del muelle
Andrómeda ¿me oyes?
estoy en el polo opuesto de todas tus prerrogativas
hago apenas esfuerzos por soltarme quizá
me arrastrara la corriente que más temo
o un chorro enceguecedor de luminarias dementes
noctilucas militantes

the ship approached slowly balancing
its stern and returning to its port of departure

I couldn't know its destiny
I didn't think it would be passing
this place where I was waiting
could it be that Argo itself
might discover this hideout
at the tip of Montevideo
where I am still bound to this writing?

stars come to rest on the mast
they flutter and shake up the deep daydream
the night is long and everything passes by close
goes on bustling about
distance is measured in pulsations
the feared trajectory is known numbered
are the palpitations subtracted from the initial sum
allotted to our hearts' accounts
Andromeda are you that sleepless nebulae or
is it me who is transiently here on earth?
the ship goes by hoisted in all its glory
over the meridian
remember: old Ptolemy catalogued the constellation with its forty-five stars in
an order similar to that of a treaty on shipbuilding modern astronomers divide
it in detail keel stern mast but only the rear half of the ship peeks in a sea
navigation chart advancing in such a way in its nocturnal course from East to
West that the stern moves forward by backing up toward the dock
Andromeda, can you hear me?
I am on the pole opposite to all of your prerogatives
I make minimal efforts at letting go perhaps
the current I fear the most would pull me
or a blinding spurt of demented luminaries
militant noctilucae

se mueve el océano invertido combado
casco protector reticulado sobre la forma
de la inteligencia
se arquea el universo en grave mitovulsión
acá las olas caen en mitad de la calle
sobre la gente que pasa despenada y sueño abajo
la marea cubre el jardín de las manzanas de oro
empuja la puerta principal la espuma se deshace
sobre la mesa de trabajo en vano estrellerío
nubes atormentadas descomponen las lejanas
Nubes de Magallanes sus tenues blancos luminosos
donde jamás encallará el Navío

acá llueve es noche cerrada
hay explosiones de miseria en cadena
minifundios de dolor y de torpeza hay barro
hay tierra hay animales hocicando
hay espesos desperdicios basurales hay
alcantarillas cloacas sumideros bocas
de tormenta tragándose el mundo de este lado
la tortura inclemente centrífuga de Andrómeda
la deriva el hundimiento del Navío aquí
en su plenitud austral y para los antiguos griegos
observadores desde el otro hemisferio levantando
sus restos en el horizonte acuoso
y el fin de Magallanes atravesado por una lanza
que lo clavó de bruces en una isla salvaje
antes de terminar la redondez del globo terráqueo

y llueve en el oscuro de veras no se ven las palmas
de las manos no hay paseo de niña ni juego
de palabras cruzadas ni viaje a Europa
ni principio tienen las cosas
en la gran avenida se ahorra energía
y en la central hidroeléctrica hay fisuras
en los muros de cemento

the ocean moves inverted warped
a protective helmet crosslinked over the shape
of intelligence
the universe bows in a deep mythovulsion
here waves break in the middle of the street
over people passing by untroubled and sleep-bound
the tide covers the garden of the golden apples
pushes open the main entrance the foam dissolves
over the worktable in a vain profusion of stars
tormented clouds upset the distant
Magellanic Clouds their tenuous luminous whites
where the ship will never run aground

here it rains the night is pitch black
there is a chain of explosions of misery
smallholdings of pain and awkwardness there is mud
there is soil there are animals rooting about
there is thick rubbish waste there are
drains sewers sinkholes storm
drains swallowing this side of the world
Andromeda's merciless centrifugal torture
the drift the sinking of the ship here
in its austral plenitude and for the Ancient Greek
contemplating from another hemisphere lifting
its remains in the aqueous horizon
and the end of Magellan pierced by a spear
that pinned him face down into a wild island
before completing the globe's circumference

it rains in the dark truly invisible are the palms
of one's hands there's no stroll for the girl nor crossword
puzzle nor trip to Europe
things even lack a beginning
in the great promenade energy is conserved
and in the hydroelectric plant cement walls
are cracked

no hay luz no se ve nada y llueve
pero me acuerdo de la luz
otros cantan conmigo de memoria la luz que
vendrá
se enfutura se esperanza se constela adentro
lanzallamas un hogar vivo amotinado
estrellas sindicadas obreras de un cielofábrica de barrio
donde se elabora destellando la historia del comienzo

there is a power outage nothing can be seen it rains
but I remember the light
others sing with me by heart the coming
light
is filled with hope it futurizes and constellates itself
flamethrower a home alive a mutinous
syndicated worker stars in a neighborhood's skyfactory
where the story of the beginning is being told in flashes

de *Composición de lugar*
y otros poemas visuales de los 70

from *Composition of Place* (1976)
and other visual poetry from the 1970s

translated by Urayoán Noel

Poniente sobre el mar del jueves 24 de febrero de 1972

Plomo derretido el aire cae
piedra el cielo cae
sobre el agua salada amarga
y negra cae
estamos para asomarnos
al pozo más profundo
las dunas se aprietan
algunas reptan
espaciosas tortugas de silencio
si lloviera habría cortocircuito
o la artillería quemaría
la espera
color de bala de metal
curtido sobre el ardor
quieto agazapado
me incrusto en mi país
en su costa amurallada
ahora es la hora
que más duele dura y fría
por si acaso
tuviéramos suerte
y pudiéramos atravesar
esa breve fisura en carne viva
así no importa
la imaginación no vale
la palabra se encanta
y también cae
estamos para callarnos
estamos para la noche.

Sea-sunset from Thursday 24 February 1972

Molten lead the air falls
stone the sky falls
over the bitter and black
saltwater it falls
we're here to peer
into the deepest well
the dunes pile in
some crawl
spacious turtles of silence
if it rained it would short circuit
or the artillery would burn
the wait
the color of a metal bullet
weathered above the still
crouched fire
I embed myself in my country
in its walled coastline
now is the time
that hurts the most hard and cold
just in case
we lucked out
and could cross
that brief fissure in the flesh
that way it doesn't matter
the imagination doesn't count
the word is enchanted
and also falls
we're here to keep quiet
we're here for the night.

Plomo derretido el aire cae

$$\frac{\text{aire plomo} \; + \; \text{cielo piedra}}{\text{agua negra}} = \text{caída}$$

$$\text{dunas} = \text{silencio}$$

$$\text{lluvia} \simeq \text{balística} \simeq \text{3ra. dimensión}$$

$$\sum \begin{array}{l} \text{a) 18 horas grises} \\ \\ \text{b) 20 horas grises} \end{array} = \text{muralla a la h. justa}$$

$$\text{muralla a la h. justa} = \text{palabra} \; - \; \big[(\text{imaginación} \; + \; \text{estrategia})\big]$$

$$\text{pesantez} = \text{terror del vuelo}$$

Molten lead the air falls

$$\frac{\text{lead air} \ + \ \text{stone sky}}{\text{black water}} = \text{fall}$$

$$\text{dunes} = \text{silence}$$

$$\text{rain} \simeq \text{ballistics} \simeq \text{3rd dimension}$$

$$\sum \begin{array}{l} \text{a) 18 gray hours} \\ \\ \text{b) 20 gray hours} \end{array} = \text{wall in the nick of tm.}$$

$$\text{wall in the nick of tm.} = \text{word} \ - \ \big[(\text{imagination} \ + \ \text{strategy})\big]$$

$$\text{weight} = \text{terror of flight}$$

Plomo   Piedra

derretido   el cielo

el aire

c   c
a   a
e   e

s   o   b   r   e

elaguasaladamargaynegra

c
a
e

p
estamos
r
asomarnos
l

pozo más profundo

así   **NO** importa
la imaginación   vale

la P A L A B R A se **E N C A N T A**

y   también

c
a
e

Lead   Stone

molten

                 the sky

the air

f   **f**
a   **a**
l   **l**
l   **l**
s   **s**

a   b   o   v   e
thebitterandblacksaltwater

                         f
                         a
     h   **l**
we're
     r   **l**
to   peer into
        h   **s**
        e

       deep   est well

Let   matter
the imagination   **NOT**   count

the W O R D is **E N C H A N T E D**
and   also

       f
       a
       l
       l
       s

Poniente sobre el mar del viernes 25 de febrero de 1972

Extenso el azul
se vuelve verde ambiguo
hacia el amarillo arisco
cercada grita la luz
a los cuatro vientos
una cadena de granadas abiertas
la enloquece
sobre el agua ciega violada
se oscurece la línea de tránsito
cerca mueren las hierbas
en la arena color uva
se sigue oyendo el grito
una y otra vez casi ahogado
rápido más rápido
ya no clama salen rayos
voces de otras luces
el aire se entumece
los médanos ofrecen
sombras plañideras
ya está consumado
ya pasó la hora.

Sea-sunset from Friday 25 February 1972

Vast blue
becomes ambiguous green
before the gruff yellow
the enclosed light cries out
to the four winds
a chain of open grenades
deranges it
above the blind violated water
the line of transit goes dark
nearby the weeds die
in the grape-colored sand
one can still hear the cry
over and over almost drowned
faster faster
it no longer calls out save for lightning
voices of other lights
the air swells
the sandbanks offer
plaintive shadows
it's already consummated
it's already time.

Extenso el azul

        cercada   enloquece
            luz

        cantera cadena castigo
                          de
               granadas

          el agua violada entreabre
líneas
piernas del tránsito
                     hasta su
        útero
        color
         uva
      la luz
    gestando
          su espectro

          su mañana

Vast blue

               enclosed   deranged
                     light

              quarry chain chastisement
                              of
                  grenades

          the violated water half-opens
lines
legs of transit
                   down to its

            grape
           colored
            uterus
        the light
gestating
              its specter

              its morning

cercada GRITA

la LUZ

N

A

cadena de granadas

e N

O

Q u

L A A A

L

e
s
ESPECTRO   ESPECTRO
E   E   E
c   S
t   P
r   E   E
o   C
    T
    R
    O

ESPECTRO

V
I
O
L
hAsta sU T R O
ESPECTRO

a
t
r
a
v
i
e L
s
a

agua

U
T
R
O

O
R
O

enclosed CRIES

the LIGHT

O

W

a chain of grenades

e R

A

G

D
o
e
s

N

SPECTER
E
E
c
t
e
r

S
P
E
C
T
E
R

S
P
E
C
T
E
R

c
r
o
s
s
the
s

V
I
dOwn to iTs
L
A
T
D

water

U
T
E
R
U
S SPECTER

O
H
E
R

49

Poniente sobre el mar del sábado 26 de febrero de 1972

Una sola fruta fugaz
desmedida.
Nadie la alcanza.
Se la traga limpiamente.
el horizonte.
El espacio es una boca
ensangrentada
vacía ahora.
Y nosotros tenemos hambre.

Sea-sunset from Saturday 26 February 1972

A lone fleeting fruit
disproportionate.
Nobody reaches her.
She is swallowed skillfully
by the horizon.
Space is a mouth
stained with blood
now empty.
And we are hungry.

Una sola fruta fugaz

sólo   viento   en   la   garganta

magra

gárgola

hambrienta

A lone fleeting fruit

only   wind   in   the   throat

meager

hungry

gargoyle

```
  S
B O C A V A C I A
  L
  A
  F U G A Z
  R
  U
  T
N A D A          Y


              V
              A
              C
        A     I
        A H O R A H O R A
        O     A
        R     M
        A     B
              R
              E
```

LONEFRUIT

MOUTH EMPTY

FLEETING

NOTHING

AND

NOWHOUR

NOW

EMPTY

1er. poniente sobre el mar del lunes 7 de enero de 1974

El día entero desde el cenit maduro
hasta la arena inerte
derrama su agua real
lava ideas transparentes
en jugo de ananá y las deja caer
sobre el mar barroco
de ola y pardo centelleo.
La gran estrella baja
insólita terrestre y marinera
empapada de tiempo alucema y briosa
atada al suave torrente
de la vasija horaria.
El agua de arriba
no se mezcla a la de abajo
algo de aceite y de vinagre
separa los dos plácidos elementos
pero la gran estrella baja
atraviesa el Aqueronte
y pasa lentamente hacia mañana.

Sea-sunset from Monday 7 January 1974

The entire day from ripe zenith
to inert sand
spills its real water
washes transparent ideas
in pineapple juice and drops them
on the baroque sea
all waves and dun sparkle.
The great star descends
unfathomable terrestrial and seafaring
soaked in lavender time and spirited
tethered to the soft torrent
of the time vessel.
The water from above
does not mix with that from below
something of oil and vinegar
separates the two calm elements
but the great star descends
crosses the Acheron
and goes slowly towards tomorrow.

2° poniente

Un renacimiento esperanzado
y loco
pero se suicida
veloz a pique
un terror incendiado
de punta
en el horizonte
una corona radiolada
le cubre la muerte
sola y luciente
sobre el ataúd.

2nd sunset

A hopeful and mad
renaissance
but it goes under
in speedy suicide
a terror ignited
on the edge
in the horizon
a jukeboxed aureole
covered by death
alone and bright
above the casket.

El día entero desde el cenit maduro

delante deja expuesta superficie

enunciación de niveles

las 20 y 30 h.

el objeto

la intemperie

o temperatura del espacio

suma
mente

solarium inteligente

detrás + allá + inseguro   lejos

auguro   pasaje
             viaje
        vía general ———>

solarium antecedente

The entire day from the ripe zenith

leaves   ahead   exposed   surface

enunciation   of   levels

20   and   30 hrs.

the object

the elements

at   space   temperature

                                    sum
                                    marily

intelligent   solarium

behind   +   there   +   uncertain   far

augur   passage
                 voyage
                 mainline ———>

antecedent   solarium

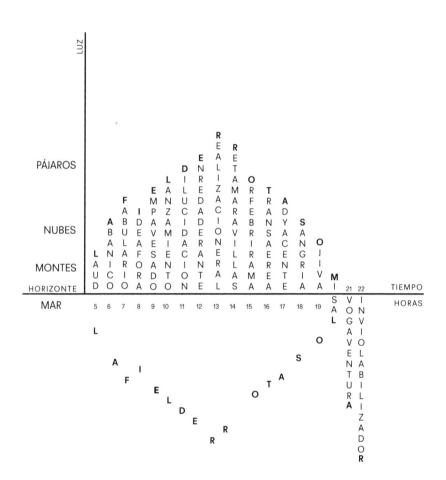

LUZ

PÁJAROS

NUBES

MONTES

HORIZONTE

MAR

TIEMPO

HORAS

5 6 7 8 9 10 11 12 13 14 15 16 17 18 19 21 22

62

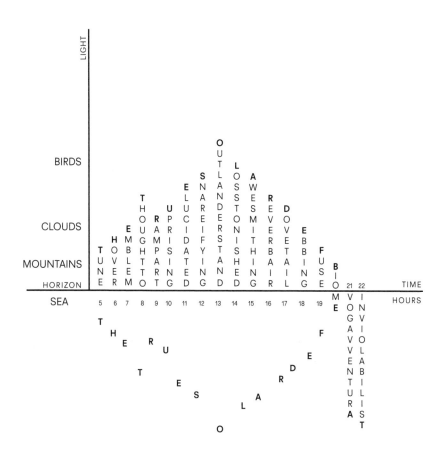

viento
viento
viento
viento
viento
viento
viento
viento
viento
viento
viento
viento
viento
viento
viento

dunadunadunadunadunaduna
dunadunadunadunadunadunaduna
dunadunadunadunadunadunadunaduna
dunadunadunadunadunadunadunadunaduna
dunadunadunadunadunadunadunadunadunaduna
dunadunadunadunadunadunadunadunadunadunaduna
dunadunadunadunadunadunadunadunadunadunadunaduna

arenaarenaarenaarenaarenaarenaarena
arenaarenaarenaarenaarenaarenaarena
arenaarenaarenaarenaarenaarenaarena
arenaarenaarenaarenaarenaarenaarena
arenaarenaarenaarenaarenaarenaarena
arenaarenaarenaarenaarenaarenaarenaarena
arenaarenaarenaarenaarenaarenaarenaarena
arenaarenaarenaarenaarenaarenaarenaarena
arenaarenaarenaarenaarenaarenaarenaarenaarena
arenaarenaarenaarenaarenaarenaarenaarenaarena
arenaarenaarenaarenaarenaarenaarenaarenaarena
arenaarenaarenaarenaarenaarenaarenaarenaarenaarena
arenaarenaarenaarenaarenaarenaarenaarenaarenaarena
arena
arena
arena
arena
arena
arena
arena
arena
arena
arena

wind
wind
wind
wind
wind
wind
wind
wind
wind
wind
wind
wind

dunedunedunedunedunedunedunedune
dunedunedunedunedunedunedunedune
dunedunedunedunedunedunedunedune
dunedunedunedunedunedunedunedunedune
dunedunedunedunedunedunedunedunedune
dunedunedunedunedunedunedunedunedunedune
dunedunedunedunedunedunedunedunedunedune
dunedunedunedunedunedunedunedunedunedunedune
dunedunedunedunedunedunedunedunedunedunedune
dunedunedunedunedunedunedunedunedunedunedunedune
dunedunedunedunedunedunedunedunedunedunedunedune
dunedunedunedunedunedunedunedunedunedunedunedunedune
dunedunedunedunedunedunedunedunedunedunedunedunedune

sandsandsandsandsandsandsand
sandsandsandsandsandsandsand
sandsandsandsandsandsandsand
sandsandsandsandsandsandsand
sandsandsandsandsandsandsand
sandsandsandsandsandsandsand
sandsandsandsandsandsandsandsand
sandsandsandsandsandsandsandsand
sandsandsandsandsandsandsandsand
sandsandsandsandsandsandsandsandsand
sandsandsandsandsandsandsandsandsand
sandsandsandsandsandsandsandsandsandsand
sandsandsandsandsandsandsandsandsandsand

sand
sand
sand
sand
sand
sand
sand
sand
sand
sand

Trazo (Derivado 1)

¿Por qué esta arena en ambar y reposo? ¿Esta piedra qué? de suave molienda? Cuerpo del desierto invadiendo la hoja donde escrito la página donde estoy signando el águila, el libro donde me emplumo de placer ¿De donde esta cáscara pálida trizada? ¿Cómo este folen estéril? Manos del desierto cubriendo el cuaderno donde inicio la marea, la mesa donde sufro humillaciones y hago mundo, la tabla donde grabo figuras de hábeas corpus. ¿Cuándo esta harina insalubre? ¿Para qué esta terrible paciencia? Gravedad del desierto sojuzgando el pliego donde amarro velas y nudos, destempladas, la memoria donde tiemblo sin medida hundida hasta la cintura en el canal del frío, el códice sombrío donde tomar razón de la ceguera.

Outline (Derivative 1)

Why this sand in amber and repose? This stone what?
a soft grind? Desert body invading the sheet where I write
the page where I'm signing the eagle, the book where
I feather myself with pleasure. From where this pale
cracked skin? How this sterile pollen? Desert hands
covering the notebook where I initiate the tide, the
table where I suffer humiliations and make worlds, the
slab on which I carve figures of habeas corpus. How long
this impure flour? Why this terrible patience? Desert
gravity subjugating the segment where I trim sails and
discordant clouds, the memory where I shiver madly,
waist-deep inside the cold canal, the dark codex in
which to acknowledge blindness.

Trazo (Derivado 2)

larga línea comienzo   y está donde otra
invadiendo trazo   pronto honda nada
donde por línea viento viento la torna   donde
                                viento que? la torna

escrito?   honda y arena está larga   sigo
duna   hay desierto
                honda la larga vez
está comprendo pero más   el otro   el viento
médano del allá
y la línea está sobre la hoja

                        no de la línea

Outline (Derivative 2)

long line beginning   and it's else where
invading   outline   soon deep nothing
where   by line   wind   wind   erases it   where
                                wind that? erases it
written?   deep and sand is long   I'm still
dune   today desert
            deep the long time
this I comprehend but more   the other   the wind
sandbank of there
and the line is on the leaf
                        not of the line

arena línea y trazo que?

        comprendo viento   y

sigo está nada escrito?   viento la sigo está nada

donde comienzo el donde   honda línea   el otro

        y   sobre   viento.

está vez allá pronto invadiendo   pero honda

la donde la y larga   línea está honda

    torra deciento   viento

una duna hay médano más no otra larga pero línea

    hoja

y la torra

Outline (Derivative 3)

sand line and outline that?
                          I comprehend   wind   and
follow this nothing written? wind I will follow it this   nothing
where I begin the where   deep line   the other
                             wind   and on
this time there soon invading   but deep
the where the and long   line is deep
                            erases desert   wind
a dune there is sandbank   more not other long but line
                            leaf

and erases it

Trazo (Derivado 4)

arden
desandan
arden

hacia   hacia
pasos   abrazos
lazos

+   **uñas**
and   **cuñas** hincadas

en riesgosa tela
piel de cristales   la   A R E N A

red   **pre**liminar
red   **pre**sentimiento
acaso **pre–**
clara   **real escapatoria ?**

túnel en el espesor del movimiento

la vida
vida ésta
tenaz

prehistoria

y caer
pido amor   el agua imprescindible
es honda la sed   un **pozo**
gozo despojos

hebras

de la sibila
hila en el viento
hila " " desierto

Outline (Derivative 4)

burning
　　　　retracing
burning

　toward　　　toward
paces　　embraces
　　　laces

　　+　　　claws
　and　　wedges　hooked

　　in dangerous fabric
　　skin of crystals　　　the　　　S A N D

　preliminary　web
　premonitory　web
　　perhaps　pre–
　eminent　actual escape ?

tunnel in the density of　movement

in　life
　life　this
　　　tenacious

　　　prehistory

and to fall
　I ask for love　　the indispensable water
　the thirst is deep　a　well
　　　　spell　spoils

　threads

of　the　sibyl
　weaving　in　the　wind
　weaving　"　"　desert

de *Identidad de ciertas frutas*

from *Identity of Certain Fruits* (1983)

translated by Anna Deeny Morales

I

(la manzana 1)

Por las manzanas
   —deliciosamente—
conozco el deseo
descubro la salud
y esa larva de muerte
que se lleva en medio del esplendor.

Ser como la manzana
    implica
     todas las culpas
pero es excitante la propuesta.
La manzana es brillante
   y peligrosa:
una sola puede incendiar un huerto.

Ser como la manzana
es estar—en la alta fiesta del día—
   toda de raso rojo y diamantes
y llevar en el índice enguantado
   un anillo de sombra.

I

(the apple 1)

By way of apples
        —deliciously—
I come upon desire
discover well-being
and that larva of death
folded in the midst of splendor.

To be as the apple
        involves
        all fault
but the proposal thrills.
The apple is brilliant
     and dangerous:
one alone can flame an orchard.

To be as the apple
is to be—at the high dance of day—
     all red satin and diamonds
and on a gloved finger wear
     a ring of dusk.

III

(la naranja)

Yace un sol poniente
    en la fuente donde brilla
        la naranja del postre.

Los gajos encendidos
y la ceniza de lo oscuro
    dan pasos en mi boca:
se encuentran en un bosque a medianoche
con los salteadores del placer
y una ácida aparición
y un terror que los sigue desde lejos.

Los gajos y mi lengua saben más que yo.

III

(the orange)

A setting sun rests
      on the tray where
           the dessert orange shines.

Blazing slices
and ashes of what dark
      round my mouth:
they're found in woods at midnight
with pleasure's thieves
an acidic apparition
and terror that from a distance hounds.

The slices and my tongue know more than I.

V

(el membrillo)

Al membrillo lo quiero y no lo quiero.
Como a una flor paralizada de pánico
                         pregunto a la fruta
—que tiene además el color de los celos—

Cae una respuesta: la locura.
Cae otra respuesta: la dureza.

Al membrillo lo quiero y no lo quiero.

Entonces viene el viento al solar del gusto
y mis dientes devastan la pulpa impenetrable
mientras por los aires quedan—echando jugos—
                         insoportables alucinaciones.

V

(the quince)

Quince is one I want and don't.
As if to a flower stiff with panic
          I ask the fruit
—that has also the color of jealousy—

An answer falls: madness.
Another answer falls: rigidity.

Quince is one I want and don't.

Then the wind arrives to the site of taste
and my teeth raze the impenetrable pulp
while through airs linger—letting liquids go—
          insufferable hallucinations.

VII

(las uvas 1)

Me gustaría beber las uvas
como bebe el cabrito su leche
de un emparrado de espuma.

Mas es tibia la leche
                              y las uvas sombrías.
Las uvas llevan alcohol parecido al de la luna
bajo el otoño todavía joven.

VII

(the grapes 1)

I'd like to drink grapes
how a kid suckles milk
from an arbor of froth.

But milk is warm
               and grapes somber.
Grapes carry a liquor like the moon's
in a still young autumn.

IX

(los higos)

Tiene sangre el fruto de la higuera
            y destila su néctar tenaz
                        su culposo jarabe
                        sigilosamente.
Ha habido un crimen
            una violación
            bajo las grandes hojas.

Yo observaba
            embebida
            a través de las ramas.
Los higos cuelgan maduros
            amoratados
            remordimientos.
                        Los higos
cuelgan del árbol
            como murciélagos de melaza
            como ahorcados
por robar un manojo de lujuria.

IX

(the figs)

The fig tree's fruit holds blood
          and distills its tenacious nectar
               its guilty syrup
               surreptitiously.

A crime was committed
        a violation
        under the wide leaves.

I watched
      drunk
      through the branches.
The ripe figs hang
        black and blue
       regrets.
                Figs
hang from the tree
         like molasses bats
         like people hanged
for robbing a fist full of lust.

X

(la granada)

La granada es una fruta
        una muñeca rusa
        un recuerdo rojizo
                  que se parte
      lleno de huevos diminutos
              de jalea carmín
   y cada huevecillo
       con pequeños pichones color fresa
   y en cada pichón rosa-vivo
       inacabables granos de marfil húmedo.

Su memoria es apenas una savia azucarada
       donde enrojece
       la sorpresa apetecible.

X

(the pomegranate)

The pomegranate is a fruit
        a Russian doll
        a reddish memory
                    you split
      full of tiny eggs
          of crimson jelly
    and each small egg
        with little strawberry-colored chicks
    and in each chick living-pink
        endless seeds of humid ivory.

Its memory is barely a sugary sap
        where the desirable surprise
        turns flush.

XIV

(el pomelo)

Identificación:
            un pomelo es una capa brillante
                        de espeso amarillo cromo
                        diluído con leche
            que configura o contiene:
            nueve gajos gigantes de menudas gotas
                                    semitransparentes,
            una taza de verano líquido,
            una llamarada de acidulado alcohol,
            una pizca de miel o benevolencia;
            tres gramos de acíbar seriamente acusados.

Temperamento:
            plácido aparente:
            soporta sueños amargos más   filosóficos
                                        que sensuales
                sostenidos por una indiferencia
                entre agria y dulce.

Referencias:
            lo han visto siempre sereno y luminoso
            parecido a una lámpara
            parecido a un libro dorado
                        lleno de láminas
            donde anidan secretas alegorías.

XIV

(the grapefruit)

Identification:
        a grapefruit is a glowing cloak
                of thick yellow chrome
                watered down with milk
        that forms or folds:
        nine sizable slices of minuscule
                translucent drops,
        a cup of liquid summer,
        a flare of alcohol acidulated,
        a pinch of honey or benevolence,
        three grams of aloe somberly accused.

Temperament:
        seemingly good-natured:
        endures bitter dreams more   philosophic
                        than sensual
          sustained by an indifference
          to sour or sweet.

References:
        noticed ever-centered and luminous
        looking like a lamp
        like a book golden
            full with illustrations
        wherein allegories nest hidden.

XVII

(el damasco)

El damasco es todo damasco:
su color su piel su textura
su terso carozo de damasco.
Tiene gustos sucesivos
          circulares
                   a damasco fresco
                   a damasco seco
                   a damasco abrillantado.
El árbol del damasco
se sueña a sí mismo.

XVII

(the apricot)

The apricot is all apricot:
its color its rind its texture
its smooth damask apricot kernel.
It holds successive circular
                pleasures
                        of fresh apricot
                        of dried apricot
                        candied apricot.
The apricot tree
dreams its own self.

XX

(las castañas 1)

Suponiendo que el árbol del sabor
fuera una aparición o un sueño
—ese árbol asombraría indefinidos paisajes—

Las castañas están a la altura del recuerdo
madurando entre el misterioso chocolate
                    la femenina batata
            y un toque suspicaz a nueces
en una calle de París
                    humildemente.

Sobre un suave hornillo se asan
los oscuros encerados frutos medievales.
Y hace frío.

XX

(the chestnuts 1)

Supposing that the tree of flavor
were an apparition or dream
—that tree would astound boundless landscapes—

Chestnuts are comparable to memory
maturing among the mysterious chocolate
                    the feminine yam
            and a suspect hint of walnut
on a Paris street
                    unassumingly.

Over a small smooth stove they roast
the dark waxed medieval fruits.
And it's cold.

XX

(las castañas 2)

En otras ramas del árbol renacen
             otras castañas.
Estamos en Montevideo.
          Verano u otoño quizá.
Miro una evanescente bombonería.
Miro las hojas de espejo con iniciales.
Detrás
en su caja bordeada de festón y puntillas
        están los capullos
           los cofres
        bajo un blanco pétalo glaceado
—la bella durmiente del bosque—
—la princesa extranjera "marron glacé"—
serenísimas y lujosas crisálidas.

Entonces vuela una extraviada imagen:
las castañas desnudas
              cubiertas de plata
resplandecen
       imposibles.

XX

(the chestnuts 2)

On other branches of the tree other
               chestnuts are born again.
We're in Montevideo.
          Maybe summer or fall.
I see an evanescent candy store.
I see the initialed mirror leaves.
Behind
in her case lined with festoon and point lace
               there the buds
                    jewel boxes
               below a white glazed petal
—the sleeping beauty of the woods—
—the foreign princess "marron glacé"—
such serene and luxuriant chrysalises.

Then a lost image glides through the air:
the naked chestnuts
                    covered in silver
they resplend
               impossibly.

de *La dama de Elche*

from *The Lady of Elche* (1987)

translated by Kristin Dykstra

"Avec les gemissements graves du Montevideen"
                                        (Lautréamont)

soy Amanda—montevideana—
hija de Amanda la de ojos de vaca
                diosa contemporánea
                corazón de mirlos con relámpagos
donde anida el rayo que quiebra la noche
        aletea la alegría la vida conmovida
y de Rimmel padre
                gallo de riña
                violento cancerbero
                o tierno migajón bajo las plumas
                casi brújulas casi flechas
hermana de Rimmel el sacrificado y querido
                        muerto porque los muertos
                        del reino de los muertos
                        lo rodearon

soy Amanda mujer de José Pedro
seguro como un cedro encrestado
                                poderoso
como la montaña

necesario y distante como el río
                que nos da de beber
no lo habitan las palabras
el viento vela su inaccesible escarpado amor

soy Amanda madre de Alvaro
                ansioso
                velero "ardiente"
fruto de la unión de ese árbol encendido
con mi escuadra de navíos derivantes

"Avec les gemissements graves du Montevideen"
(Lautréamont)

I'm Amanda—from Montevideo—
daughter of Amanda, cow-eyed
                    contemporary deity
                    blackbird heart with lightning bolts
where the flash that shatters night comes to roost
        it flaps joy inciting life
daughter of Rimmel, father
                    fighting cock
                    cruel Cerberus
                    or tender marrow under the feathers
                    almost bearings almost arrows
sister of Rimmel sacrificed and dear
                    dead because the dead
                    from the kingdom of the dead
                    surrounded him

I'm Amanda wife of José Pedro
steady as a cedar, lofty
                        potent
as the mountain

necessary and distant as the river
                        that gives us drink
words do not live there
wind veils its love, escarped, inaccessible

I'm Amanda mother of Alvaro
                    anxious
                    "ardent" sailboat
fruit of the union of that burning tree
with my squadron of drifting ships

anunciado por un pichón de golondrina
que cayó sobre mis piernas una tarde de febrero
y vivió en mi casa
        revoloteó junto a mi cama
        comió insectos
y a los nueve días desapareció

soy Amanda
        y voy hacia Amanda sin destino
          apátrida
perseguida por un tábano dorado
en medio de la púrpura
        de un empecinado y continuo
        asesinato de Amanda

announced by a baby swallow
who fell on my legs one February afternoon
and lived in my house
                    fluttered by my bed
                    ate insects
and disappeared on the ninth day

I'm Amanda
                and I move toward Amanda without a destination
                            stateless
chased by a golden horsefly
through the purple
            of an inexorable continuous
            murder of Amanda

(the painted desert and the petrified forest)

los mismos fantasmas velan en Tebas
o en el Bosque Petrificado

pasa Edipo ciego lo veo titubeando entre
las ruinas inexistentes de su ciudad
                    en la alucinada Hélade
y aparecen José Pedro y Amanda
            espejismos del Desierto Pintado
            vagan los tres—se imaginan—
sobre la yacente y pétrea arboleda
cegados por la misma humareda perpetua

        los cascos de la luna
                    su caballo blanco
                    anduvo por allí
        los troncos muestran sus ágatas perfectas
        sus huellas de sueño sin presagios

somos sólo espectros de luz rayos de la memoria

(the painted desert and the petrified forest)

the same phantoms keep watch in Thebes
or the Petrified Forest

blind Oedipus passes by I see him hesitating among
nonexistent ruins of his city
                    in hallucinatory Hellas
and José Pedro appears with Amanda
        mirages in the Painted Desert
        the three wander—so they imagine—
over the sprawled, petrified grove of trees
blinded by the same everpresent cloud of smoke

        the quarters of the moon
                                its white horse
                                walked this ground
        trunks display their flawless agates
        their tracks in unforetold dream

we're only spectra of light, rays of memory

(la dama de Elche)

consumiendo los telares del Prado
a lo largo de opulentas galerías
cuando recorría los comedores del color
                    las cocinas de la forma
bajé hasta la arcaica oreja de la piedra
allá en el subsuelo cerca de Elche mediterránea

entonces mi cabeza se puso a escuchar
                    apretada
                    atenta
entre dos ruedas
entre dos caracoles marinos
entre dos manos de piedra
entre dos ajustados certeros auriculares

paladas de cal apagada
golpes secos de blanco
recuerdos del oxígeno
movían las ruedas con engarces
                    o alvéolos vacíos

un ruido sordo espantable y terrestre
(había explotado ya la bomba de Hiroshima
en el pezón inicial del planeta)
se vertía lentamente   por los ojos
                    por las fisuras de la nariz
                    por la ranura cerrada
                            de los labios

toda la piedra se hizo caverna
oreja resonante
                    y yo era esa oreja resonante
ese pabellón acústico de mineral alimenticio
                    arrojado al azar

(the Lady of Elche)

taking in textiles at the Prado
moving through opulent galleries
touring canteens of color
          kitchens of form
I descended to the archaic auricle of stone
there underground near Mediterranean Elche

then my head began to channel attention
                    squeezed
                    alert
between two wheels
between two seashells
between two stone hands
between two tightfitting accurate auriculars

spadefuls of slaked lime
dry white blows
memories of oxygen
turned the wheels through settings
                         or empty alveoli

a terrible terrestrial deaf sound
(the Hiroshima bomb had already blown up
at the planet's nipple and origin)
was slowly dumping   through the eyes
                         through fissures of the nose
                         through the closed slot
                              for the lips

all stone became cavern
ringing ear
          and I was that ringing ear
acoustic pavilion in nourishing mineral
                    cast at random

.

escultura forma ibérica piedra caliza
Reina mora oyente pagana
                              radioescucha
oigo los pasos de los incas
bajando las escaleras de Machu Picchu

los auriculares a los lados de la cara
                    eran cucharas profundas
                              remolinos temporales

yo estaba afuera y los miraba
                    y caía hacia el fondo
atraída al borde del peligro

yo estaba afuera y adentro
era la espectadora y el museo
era la piedra y su caverna y su oreja

suenan tambores y oboes y voy con ellos
y entro con los ruidos de la calle
                    de la casa
con el zumbido de un motor en marcha
entro con la muchedumbre vociferante
es un torrente la quemazón de las noticias
entrando por el oído redondo
                              a todo volumen

más tarde sentí que salía por sus ojos
el aleteo asordinado de una torcaza
                    en el espacio baldío
salía con el silencio
        envuelto en un lienzo aceitado
salía con la señora sombra
salía con la dama de Elche de la mano
los demás huecos de la cara
—acompañantes—arrojaron apariciones

Iberian form sculpture limestone chunk
Moorish Queen pagan listener
                              I tune in
to hear the footsteps of the Inca
descending the stairs at Machu Picchu

the auriculars on each side of my face
                    were deep spoons
                            temporal eddies

I was outside looking at them
                    and falling toward the bottom
pulled toward the edge of danger

I was outside and inside
spectator and museum
stone its cavern and its ear

drums and oboes play I move with them
and enter with the noises of the street
                        the house
to the hum of a running motor
I enter with the vociferous crowd
a stream the burn from the news
entering the round inner ear
                            at full blast

later I felt myself leaving through her eyes
muffled flapping of a ringdove
                    through wasteland
leaving with the silence
        wrapped in an oiled canvas
leaving with mistress shadow
leaving, Lady of Elche by the hand
other holes in the face
—escorts—they cast apparitions

la luz ofrece su único alimento
       luz magra y ritual
para el ángulo de las tomas
                y el encuadre
de una cámara fotográfica al acecho

light offers its only fuel
        a lean and ritual light
for the angles of shots
               and frames
by a camera waiting to spring its trap

(día de lluvia)

¿qué hacías Ramón Berenguer señor de Elche
       hijo de Jaime II de Aragón
      en el año 1300 y pico
un día de lluvia como hoy
en medio de las palmas datileras
que rodeaban aquella ciudad con alminares?

¿acaso orinabas al viento
       —igual que el joven Arturo Rimbaud—
de espaldas a las huestes feudales
con el asentimiento de las altas palmeras?

las palmas datileras crecían
sobre la dama de Elche enterrada
sin que nadie lo supiera
y cuando caía un dátil
       caía un trozo de juventud
          levemente

juventud sobre juventud
       Berenguer sobre Berenguer
caían en silenciosa batalla sobre la dama de Elche

cubierta por densas colonias de asombro
mientras iba perdiendo sus colores
y bebía sorbo a sorbo
       el jugo de las raíces de la palma
en profundos tazones de dibujo griego
o con asas de cuello de cisnes romanos
o en jarras de bronce que los árabes labran
sepultados bajo relojes de arcilla interminable

lágrimas dulces—intensos dátiles azules—
mojan toda la tierra

(day of rain)

what were you doing Ramón Berenguer, Lord of Elche
                son of James II of Aragon
                in the year 1300 something
on a day of rain like today
among the date palms
that circled the city with minarets?

maybe you were pissing into the wind
                —just like young Arthur Rimbaud—
your back to the feudal armies
with approval from the tallest palms?

the date palms grew
above the buried Lady of Elche
although no one knew it
and when a date would fall
                a fragment of youth would fall
                        gently

youth over youth
                Berenguer over Berenguer
they fell in noiseless battle above the Lady of Elche

covered by dense colonies of wonderment
as she gradually lost her colors
and sip by sip drank
        juice from the roots of the palm
from deep bowls with Greek patterns
or handles like the necks of Roman swans
or bronze jars wrought by Arabs
buried under endless clockwork silt

sweet tears—dates intensely blue—
moisten the whole of the earth

hoy llueve   aquí en Montevideo
                sin pausa
                sin prisa
el aire es un velamen extenso y leve
lo empujan los dedos húmedos de la perspectiva
hacia la lejana
                española Elche desierta y blanca
y como si se mirara bajo el agua
tiembla este muro cercano
                por donde sube la hiedra verde
                empapada
llueve en el jardín de mi casa
caen las gotas en manojos persistentes

los días chorrean de las gárgolas memoriosas
y corren por las calles de mi ciudad
acaudalando el río de piel mestiza
                Río de la Plata

miro llover en presente
                en suspenso
observo mi rostro detenido un instante
en la luz del combate cuerpo a cuerpo
también soy Berenguer
                de este lado de la pantalla
                en este nuevo mundo
por el cine a tientas pasan torrentes luminosos
mechas encendidas chisporrotean
                acercándose al clímax

hoy se podrían comenzar a filmar
los sueños del universo
la biografía en cámara lenta
                de una crisálida
cambiando sus transparencias

it's raining today   here in Montevideo
                   unceasing
                   unhurried
the air is a vast delicate membrane
damp perspectival fingers push it
into Spain's distant
                  Elche, deserted and white
and seen as if underwater
this nearby wall shivers
               where green ivy climbs
               dripping wet
it's raining in the garden at my house
drops fall in persistent scatters

days drip off memorious gargoyles
and run through the streets of my city
accumulating in the mestizo river
                 the River Plate

I watch it rain in present tense
                   suspended
I observe my face arrested for an instant
in the light of hand to hand combat
I too am Berenguer
                   on this side of the screen
                   in this new world
luminous torrents grope their way through the theater
highlights spark, ignited
                   approaching the climax

today they could begin to film
dreams of the universe
the slow motion biography
               of a chrysalis
changing its transparencies

se superponen finísimas películas
                    apenas esfumadas
para los jardines bajo la lluvia de Debussy

miro llover
miro brillar la mirada
                    desprovista de yelmo
                                    de escudo
                                    de guantes
vibrando a través de otras mirillas
que se entreabren y cierran
                                    con sigilo
¿qué esperas ahora caballero feudal
                    sobreviviente bajo la lluvia
                    aparecido
en este espacio familiar?

por el jardín de mi casa
pasa muy cerca
                    casi comiendo azúcar de mi mano
                    tu caballo color humo

for the gardens under Debussy's rain
slender superimposed films
        almost melt away

I watch it rain
watch the gaze gleam
        deprived of helmet
          of shield
          of gloves
vibrating through other peepholes
that open halfway then shut
           surreptitiously
what are you waiting for now, feudal knight
        survivor in the rain
        apparition
in this familial space?

he passes very close by
at the garden in my house
        almost eating sugar from my hand:
        your horse the shade of smoke

de *Con el tigre entre las cosas*

from ***With the Tiger Among My Things*** (1986-1994)

translated by Jeannine Marie Pitas

De gatos y pájaros

1

El gato saltó sobre los pájaros.
Y todos huyeron
menos uno que no era pájaro.

2

Cuando encuentro un pájaro
me le subo a las alas sin preguntarle
y vuelo entre heliotropos.
A la tarde me bajo
entro en la cocina
y le doy de comer al gato
un pajarito envuelto
en papel de plomo:
en ese pasamos los días
el pájaro, el gato y yo.

3

Mi gato amarillo cazaba pájaros por placer
luego los traía entre los dientes sin apretarlos
y con un sordo maullido nervioso los depositaba
paralizados de miedo
sobre la alfombra del comedor

primero:
para que yo fuera su testigo y su cómplice,
segundo:
para que el pájaro tratara de huir
sutilmente custodiado por su salto

Of Cats and Birds

1

The cat jumped over the birds.
And they all flew away
except for the one that wasn't a bird.

2

When I meet a bird
I climb onto its wings without asking
and I fly among the heliotropes.
In the afternoon I come down
enter the kitchen
and feed the cat
a little bird wrapped
in aluminum foil:
this is how we spend our days—
the bird, the cat and me.

3

My yellow cat hunted birds for pleasure
later he'd carry them between his teeth without squeezing them
and with a deaf nervous meow he'd deposit them
paralyzed with fear
on top of the dining room rug

first:
so I might be his witness and accomplice,
second:
so that the bird might try to flee
subtly guarded by his leap

mientras él soportaba en un temblor
esa sensación de poder exquisito.

4

Sostengo en el mismo plano
un pájaro vivo con la cabecita rosa hacia abajo
al lado de otro
con la cabecita violeta hacia arriba
como el poniente—dijo uno
como la aurora—murmuró el otro
corridos un poco para que las alas de uno
se ajusten levemente con las alas del otro.

A los dos los ato
por las puntas de las plumas
con finísimos hilos de oro
y los suelto
en el aire el vuelo luminoso y sombrío
relampagueante
queda en suspenso

uno canta / el otro calla /
uno mira al Norte / el otro al Sur
uno es feliz / el otro desdichado /
pero me parece que saben quien soy
y siento como una secreta compartida
disposición de ánimo.

5

Para el gato media docena de gorriones
pueden hacerle volar el mundo.

while he, trembling, might endure
that feeling of exquisite power.

4

On the same plane, I hold
a live bird with its little pink head downwards
and another
with its little purple head upwards
like the west wind—said the one
like the dawn—murmured the other
fluttering a bit so the wings of the one
lightly balance the wings of the other.

I tie both of them
by the tips of their feathers
with the tiniest gold threads
and I release them
in the air, the luminous, shadowy flight
flashingly
remains suspended

one sings / the other is quiet
one looks to the North / the other to the South
one is happy / the other hapless
but it seems to me that they know who I am
and I sense a secret, shared
disposition of the spirit.

5

For the cat, a half dozen sparrows
are enough to make the world fly in his direction.

6

Al tigre le gusta la paloma
y la paloma tiembla,
pero ser paloma es una apasionante recompensa.

7

De tanto soñar con los pájaros
aquel gato acurrucado sobre la cama
tenía la indolencia de un almohadón lleno de plumas.

8

Al pájaro le falta astucia
no ha conseguido nunca esconderse detrás del gato.

9

Cuando apenas por un instante
dejaba escapar al pájaro
el gato lo mantenía atado
como si remontara una cometa
luego el salto sorpresivo recogía el hilo
y el pájaro retornaba de golpe
para volver a empezar.

10

¿Dónde están enterradas las palomas?
Nunca he visto palomas muertas.

11

Esta bandada de palomas da vueltas sobre mi casa
como un helicóptero /

6

The tiger likes the dove
and the dove trembles
but to be a dove is an enthralling reward.

7

After so much dreaming about birds
that cat curled up on the bed
he was as lazy as a big pillow stuffed with feathers.

8

The bird has no guile
he has never managed to hide from the cat.

9

When, for barely an instant
The cat let a bird escape,
he kept him tied
flying him like a kite
later with a surprise leap he grabbed the string
and the bird instantly returned
to do it all over again.

10

Where are the doves buried?
I've never seen dead doves.

11

That flock of doves flies in circles over my house
like a helicopter /

en cada una de sus amplias vueltas
los álamos se deshojan
y dejan caer una lluvia amarilla predestinada.

12

El cardenal enjaulado se daba impulsivo
contra los rígidos alambres:
era como si me fuera a salir del pecho.

13

El pájaro sobre la última rama
de la hiedra que trepa por el muro
cambia de idea
(un salto imperceptible)
y se echa a volar
y cambia de dominios
de color
de situación
de límites:
en ese punto del salto
está siempre la palabra poética.

14

Sólo en su propio territorio
el tigre puede atrapar a la paloma:

cuando la paloma vuela
quedan modificadas las reglas de la caza.

in each of its full rounds
the poplars forfeit some leaves
and let loose a predestined yellow rain.

12

The caged cardinal grew impulsive
against those rigid wires:
it was as if she were about to burst out from my chest.

13

The bird on the last branch
of ivy climbing the wall
changes his plan
(an indiscernible jump)
and sets off flying
and alters his dominions
of color
of situation
of limits
at that point, in that jump
the poetic word is always present.

14

Only in its own territory
can the tiger trap the dove:

when the dove flies
the rules of the hunt are altered.

15

(variaciones sobre otros mirlos)

I was of three minds,
like a tree
in which there are three blackbirds.
                    Wallace Stevens

Miro uno dos tres mirlos
pinto tres mirlos
deshilo el tejido
deshilo el tejido el nido
el tríptico (mirlos):
negro no
color espejo no
azul plata no
tres tonos
tres ramas ardientes:
un solo mirlo

miro uno dos tres mirlos
pinto tres mirlos
enhebro el tejido
tejo el sonido
tejo el nido
el tríptico (mirlos):
negro sí
color espejo sí
azul plata sí
tres tonos
tres ramas ardientes:
ningún mirlo.

15

(variations on other blackbirds)

I was of three minds
like a tree
in which there are three blackbirds.
                    Wallace Stevens

I see one two three blackbirds
I paint three blackbirds
I unravel the fabric
I unravel the fabric the nest
the triptych (blackbirds):
not black
not mirror-colored
not blue silver
three tones
three burning branches:
one single blackbird

I see one two three blackbirds
I paint three blackbirds
I thread the fabric
I weave the sound
I weave the noise
the triptych (blackbirds):
yes black
yes mirror-colored
yes blue silver
three tones
three burning branches:
not one single blackbird.

Las plantas y el audio

1

En el comedor de mi casa
hay un sistema electrónico
que habla en voz baja
a las plantas en maceta.

Entonces: la Amaranta
y la Espada de San Jorge,
la Dracena y el Palo de agua,
copulan escandalosamente
a la hora en que la Cenicienta
pierde su zapato.

2

La Dracena—como hembra del Dragón—
usa sombrero de plumas rojas.

Cuando suena el audio
se pone de cabeza y ejecuta el break-dance
y su compañero el Palo de Agua
desesperado
tira sus lazos de clorofila
y le da de beber un dedal de ajenjo helado
mientras le dice:
—Dracena, préstame el rojo y te doy el verde.

La Dracena grita tan agudo que no se la oye.
Una llamarada recoge el sombrero
sale corriendo
se precipita

The Plants and the Audio

1

In my dining room
there's an electronic system
that speaks in low tones
to the plants in their pots.

And so: the Amaranth
and St. George's Sword
the Dracaena and the Water Cornstalk
have scandalous sex
at the very moment when Cinderella
loses her shoe.

2

The Dracaena—female Dragon
wears a hat of red feathers.

When the audio sounds
she stands on her head and performs a break-dance
and her partner, the Water Cornstalk
desperate
tosses out his chlorophyll lassos
and offers her a thimble of iced absinth
while he says:
—Dracaena, lend me the red one and I'll give you the green one.

The Dracaena screams so shrilly that no one can hear her.
A sudden blaze snatches her hat
takes off running
plunges

y se ahoga.
Se extiende por la habitación un tul vaporoso:
unas hebras de incendio sofocado.

3

La enrojecen los celos. La Dracena piensa:
la Amaranta lleva en sus hojas las señales
que le dejó la Espada de San Jorge;
una líneas intensas
como si la hubieran besado deslizándose
incisivamente.

La Dracena piensa en la Espada de San Jorge.

Cuando duerme abre los brazos como llamaradas
y se queda esperando el filo delicioso.

4

La Amaranta se acurruca.
La sombra rápida
entrecortada
de la música,
la cubre de rayas.
Es una gata verde-azul-añil sicodélica
cuando siente
que la Espada de San Jorge
se le acerca.

La Espada desea la Amaranta.

La Amaranta se encierra
entre sus hojas afelpadas,
obscenamente,
y tararea "blues".

and drowns.
A light tulle spreads over the room:
a few threads of smothered flame.

3

Jealousy makes her redden. The Dracaena thinks:
the Amaranth bears all the signs
that St. George's Sword left on her leaves;
some fierce lines
as if they had kissed, gliding
cuttingly.

The Dracaena thinks about St. George's Sword.

When she sleeps, she opens her arms like flames
and waits for that delicious blade.

4

The Amaranth curls herself up.
The music's quick
faltering
shadow
covers her in stripes.
She's a psychedelic green-blue-indigo cat
when she senses
the approach
of St. George's Sword.

The Sword wants the Amaranth.

The Amaranth locks herself in
among her velvety leaves,
obscenely,
and hums the blues.

5

Si se mira el Palo de Agua desde abajo
y se lo observa crecer

se diría que es generoso
y que alcanzará hasta el cielo.

Pero la Dracena lo seduce
lo llena de quemaduras
y él sufre de una sedienta fascinación.

El Palo de Agua está perdido por la Dracena.

La Dracena desnuda—sólo con collares—
no imagina que en cualquier momento
el Palo de Agua desbordado podría matarla.

La Dracena juega con el Palo de Agua
y lo roza apenas
con sus lentos labios encendidos.

El Palo de Agua hierve:
El rock le sube la savia.

6

El Palo de Agua es estudioso. Ecologista.
Memorizador del viento y la música.

A la Amaranta le gusta.
Le gusta estudiar juntos,
hacer el amor de otra manera,
y saborear despacio la lluvia.

5

If you look at the Water Cornstalk from below
and watch him growing

you might call him generous
and assert that he will reach the sky.

But the Dracaena seduces him
covers him with burn marks
and he suffers from a thirsty fascination.

The Water Cornstalk has lost his head over the Dracaena.

The naked Dracaena—only wearing necklaces—
has no idea that at any moment
the overflowing Water Cornstalk might kill her.

The Dracaena plays with the Water Cornstalk
gently brushing against him
with her slow, inflamed lips.

The Water Cornstalk boils:
Rock music raises his sap.

6

The Water Cornstalk is studious. An ecologist.
Memorizer of wind and music.

The Amaranth likes him.
She likes when they study together,
their own way of making love,
as they slowly savor the rain.

7

Ya tuvo bajo su hoja el Gran Dragón.

La Espada de San Jorge cayó sobre la Amaranta.
La Amaranta siente la hoja atigrada que la penetra.
Los azules y los "blues" cantan, gritan, deliran.
La Amaranta se olvida de todo.

La Amaranta cree que es Madonna
y que lleva en sus brazos tatuados
un corazón verde como la luz de un semáforo.
San Jorge y Michael Jackson se le confunden.

8

La Amaranta y la Dracena beben licuados
y mastican chicles durante la siesta.

A veces la Dracena pregunta:
—Amaranta ¿cuál es tu sueño preferido?

La Dracena pregunta sólo para molestar
a la Amaranta.
La Dracena sabe que la Amaranta sueña
con el caballero armado que mata al dragón.

9

La Dracena usa la lengua como hojas
como guantes.

La Dracena lleva violetas alcohólicas en la boca.

La Espada de San Jorge la espera, tenaz,
desenvainada,
pronta para la danza.

7

It already had the Great Dragon under its leaf.

St. George's Sword fell on top of the Amaranth.
The Amaranth senses the striped leaf penetrating her.
Blue hues and blues music sing, shout, rave.
The Amaranth forgets everything.

The Amaranth thinks she's Madonna
and that underneath her tattooed arms
lies a heart as green as the gleam of a traffic light.
St. George gets taken for Michael Jackson.

8

The Amaranth and the Dracaena drink milkshakes
and chew gum during the siesta.

Sometimes the Dracaena asks,
—Amaranth, what's your favorite dream?

The Dracaena asks this just to pick on
the Amaranth.
The Dracaena knows the Amaranth dreams
of a knight in shining armor who kills the dragon.

9

The Dracaena uses her tongue like leaves
like gloves.

The Dracaena carries alcoholic violets in her mouth.

St. George's Sword waits for her, persistent,
unsheathed,
ready for the dance.

10

    —Vamos, vamos,
que suena la música.
Que tocan rock.

El ritmo caliente
hace trepidar
el piso del comedor.
El aire tiembla.
El epicentro está en los ijares briosos
de las guitarras eléctricas.

Cuando cae la lámpara
las plantas crecen rapidísimo
en tomas cinematográficas aceleradas
y se injertan
en los lugares más húmedos y sedosos.

10

    —Let's go, let's go,
the music is blasting.
They're playing rock.

The hot rhythm makes
the dining room floor
vibrate.
The air shivers.
The epicenter lies in the jaunty flanks
of electric guitars.

When the lamp falls
the plants grow so fast
in accelerated cinematographic seizures
and they graft themselves
in the silkiest, most humid places.

Estudio de arrugas:
Aportes para una cosmetología

1)

Las arrugas de mis partes superiores confluyen hacia el centro del pecho: las de la cara bajan desde la frente, bordean los ojos y la nariz, rodean la boca y se descuelgan por el pescuezo. Se reúnen allí donde se juntan los senos y se introducen por debajo formando un silencioso cauce subterráneo que va a parar a la punta del corazón.

Las arrugas inferiores van hacia el monte de Venus, hacia la caverna que está en su base y trepan desde los muslos y se acercan desde el bajo vientre y la cintura, atraídas por el remolino de la antigua cueva del nacimiento.

Un niño dibujaría sobre mi cuerpo un sol alto con tiza amarilla de rayos ondulantes como filamentos en el pecho, y otro sol caído con gruesos trazos desparejos y cortos de crayola violeta, donde comienzan las piernas.

Pero un caballo no pisaría esos dos tembladerales si mi cuerpo fuera la pradera.

La luna sola bajaría la cabeza y derramaría azúcar azul sobre los dos sangrientos relojes.

2)

Las arrugas de los ojos tienen "no me olvides",
las de la boca "siemprevivas",
las de la frente marcas de las mareas.

3)

Una arruga puede ser: gusano de seda
                        germen de trigo
                        baba del diablo.

A Study of Wrinkles:
Contributions to the Field of Cosmetology

1)

The wrinkles of my upper parts converge at the center of my chest: the ones on my face descend from the forehead, skirt around the eyes and nose, encircle the mouth and trickle down the neck. They meet there where the breasts come together and insert themselves underneath, forming a silent underground gully that only stops at the tip of the heart.

The lower wrinkles go toward the Mound of Venus, toward the cavern at its base and climb up from the thighs and come together between the lower belly and the waist, drawn to the whirlpool of that ancient birthing cave.

A child would draw a high, yellow-chalk sun on my body with wavy rays like threads on my chest, and another fallen sun with thick, short, uneven, violet crayon strokes at the spot where my legs begin.

But, if my body were a grassland, no horse would step on those two quagmires.

The lone moon would lower its head and spill blue sugar over the two bleeding clocks.

2)

The wrinkles around the eyes have "forget-me-nots,"
the ones near the mouth have "cobweb houseleeks"
the ones on the forehead, the tides' watermarks.

3)

A wrinkle can be: silkworm
               wheatgerm
               devil's drool.

4)

Una arruga entre las cejas: un alfil,
dos arrugas: dos ahorcados,
tres arrugas al costado de los ojos:
        una rejilla para ver el revés.

5)

Cuando muevo la mano crecen de prisa las arrugas de los dedos. El lápiz, sostenido entre el índice, el pulgar y el mayor, las domestica como si fuera el látigo del domador.

6)

Con las arrugas de toda la piel se podría hacer un cesto resistente, una barquilla para un montgolfiero que navegara el espacio del tiempo.

7)

Las gruesas arrugas del cuello, "ahorcan pero no aprietan".

8)

Las arrugas son las pajitas con las que hace su nido la vejez.

9)

Una arruga tiene dos direcciones: la misma arruga marca el fin de la fiesta y el comienzo del día.

10)

El sueño no deja crecer arrugas: las sopla suavemente.

4)

A wrinkle between the eyebrows: a bishop,
two wrinkles: two hangmen,
three wrinkles at the sides of the eyes:
            a screen that lets you look back.

5)

When I move my hand, the wrinkles on my fingers grow quickly. The pencil, held
between the index finger, thumb and middle finger, domesticates these wrinkles
like the lion tamer's whip.

6)

With all the skin's wrinkles you could make a strong basket, a Montgolfier basket
that would sail through the space of time.

7)

The thick wrinkles of the neck "strangle but do not squeeze."

8)

Wrinkles are the straw from which old age builds its nest.

9)

One wrinkle has two positions: the same wrinkle marks the party's end and the
day's beginning.

10)

Sleep doesn't allow wrinkles to grow: it gently blows on them.

11)

Para las arrugas no hay cosmético más eficaz que la drástica muerte. Ésta las borra del cuerpo presente en apenas una hora.

12)

Las mujeres odian las arrugas porque ocupan todo el lugar disponible del espejo.

13)

Una arruga es más peligrosa que una picadura.

14)

En las palmas de las manos y en las plantas de los pies, las arrugas se reúnen para saber quienes somos.

15)

Las arrugas se encuentran en diminutos semicírculos en la yema de los dedos, o se alinean en grupos paralelos entre las falanges o se cruzan como arroyos profundos en el hueco de las palmas. Si se observan cuidadosamente las manos, las arrugas cuentan toda nuestra historia con pelos y señales.

16)

Los niños no tienen arrugas: tienen caprichos.

17)

Las arrugas no se improvisan. Son los abuelos los que contagian las arrugas a los niños y los niños las llevan en la piel tan livianas que no se ven. Cuando pasa la primavera se hacen visibles: el primer recuerdo y la primera arruga.

11)

There's no cosmetic more effective against wrinkles than drastic death. This erases them from the body in barely an hour.

12)

Women hate wrinkles because they consume all the mirror's available space.

13)

A wrinkle is more dangerous than a sting.

14)

In the palms of the hands, on the bottoms of the feet, wrinkles meet and find out who we are.

15)

Wrinkles can be found in minute semicircles on the fingertips, or they align themselves in parallel groups between the phalanx bones or they cross like deep streams in the palms' hollows. If you observe the hands carefully, you'll see that wrinkles tell our entire story in hairs and signs.

16)

Children don't have wrinkles: they have birthmarks.

17)

Wrinkles aren't improvised. Grandparents are the ones who spread wrinkles to their grandchildren, and these children bear them on the skin, so light that they can't be seen. When spring ends they become visible: the first memory and the first wrinkle.

18)

Por las arrugas de los ojos una mujer parece un pájaro,
por las arrugas de las piernas parece un elefante,
por las arrugas de las manos parece un mono.
Por las arrugas una mujer es una quimera de una especie doméstica.

19)

Los hombres sin arrugas parecen lampiños.

20)

Los jóvenes llevan las arrugas como un tenue almanaque a flor de piel.

21)

Las arrugas siempre me dicen lo que hicieron.

22)

No hay arruga sin oficio propio.

23)

A veces las arrugas, cuando se encuentran con otras, cambian de parecer.

24)

No son lo mismo las benignas, horizontales, arrugas de la frente cuando están solas, que cuando se trenzan con las cortas, verticales y hurañas del entrecejo. En ese momento la lucha por el territorio de la expresión hace que la parte superior de la cara entre en chisporroteo, como si ocurriera un cortocircuito.

La crisis pasa más o menos rápido según el gesticulador.

18)

The wrinkles of the eyes make a woman look like a bird,
the wrinkles of the legs make her look like an elephant,
the wrinkles of the hands make her look like a monkey.
Thanks to these wrinkles, a woman is a domestic sort of chimera.

19)

Men without wrinkles look hairless.

20)

Young people carry their wrinkles out in the open like a flimsy almanac.

21)

Wrinkles always tell me what they've done.

22)

There is no wrinkle without its own occupation.

23)

Sometimes wrinkles, when meeting others, change their minds.

24)

The mild horizontal wrinkles of the forehead are not the same when alone as they
are when braided with the short, vertical, hostile ones between the eyebrows. In
that moment the fight for territory of expression causes the upper part of the face
to sizzle as if short-circuiting.
The crisis passes more or less quickly according to the gesturer.

Es lo más común que, más abajo, las arrugas hastiadas de los lados de la boca, estén crispadas y atentas, o acompañen la disputa activamente.

25)

Hay arrugas que le ponen rayos a los ojos: al comienzo encienden la mirada, y después la queman.

26)

Las mujeres saben que el exterminio de una arruga cualquiera puede costarle "un ojo de la cara".

27)

Las arrugas exprimen la fruta de la boca sin piedad hasta convertirla en un ollejo.

28)

Lo bueno que tienen las arrugas del cuello es que cuando nos decapitan ya no podemos perder la cabeza.

29)

A medida que se frunce el ojal de la boca, las mujeres se vuelven más conversadoras, y lo que es peor, así consiguen estirarlo y fruncirlo mucho más.

30)

Una arruga que se ejercita es una arruga temible.

It usually happens that, farther down, the worn-out wrinkles at the sides of the mouth become tense and alert, or they actively join in the argument.

25)

There are wrinkles that give the eyes rays: at first they light up the gaze, and later they burn it.

26)

Women know that the extermination of any wrinkle can cost "an arm and a leg."

27)

Wrinkles mercilessly squeeze the mouth's fruit until it turns into that fruit's skin.

28)

The good thing about neck wrinkles is that by the time they decapitate us we can't lose our heads.

29)

As their lips' buttonholes are pursed, women become more talkative, and the worst thing is that afterwards they just stretch and purse them even more.

30)

A wrinkle in training is a wrinkle to be feared.

31)

Las orejas se arrugan menos porque no tienen nada que hacer.

Los sonidos entran sin que la oreja haga nada.

La boca, en cambio, se arruga porque trabaja mucho: abre y cierra la puerta todo el día: es portera de los víveres y portera de las palabras.

Los párpados son porteros especializados de la luz que entra y de la mirada que sale. Los párpados se arrugan mucho más: tienen el oficio de los guardianes de faro sobre el mar.

32)

Las arrugas que los hombres llevan del otro lado de la piel se llaman manías.

33)

Las pequeñas manías son arrugas internas, con forma de monos amaestrados, de donde se deduce que las arrugas y los adiestramientos son la misma cosa.

34)

Los maestros de los monos tienen numerosas arrugas y una sola manía: adiestrar a los monos, lo que quiere decir que no se sabe dónde empieza y dónde termina el mono.

35)

Dicen que el pensamiento arruga la frente, y la lujuria no sólo la boca.

36)

Una arruga es infalible en su determinación o propósito de promocionar cumpleaños.

31)

The earlobes have fewer wrinkles because they don't have anything to do.

They can do nothing, and the sound still comes in.

The mouth, on the other hand, gets wrinkled because it works so hard: it opens and closes the door all day long: it's the porter for supplies and the porter for words.

The eyelids are specialized porters for the light that comes in and the gaze that comes out. Eyelids get much more wrinkled: they have the task of guarding the lighthouse on the sea.

32)

The wrinkles that men wear on the inside of their skin are called obsessions.

33)

The little obsessions are internal wrinkles in the form of trained monkeys, from which it follows that wrinkles and training are the same thing.

34)

The monkeys' teachers have abundant wrinkles and one single obsession: to train monkeys. Therefore, it remains unknown where the monkey begins and ends.

35)

They say that thinking wrinkles the forehead, and lust wrinkles more than just the lips.

36)

A wrinkle is infallible in its resolve, its constant purpose of promoting birthdays.

37)

A uno le gustaría sacarse de la mitad de las arrugas por la cabeza, como un buzo de lana, y la otra mitad por los pies, como si fuera una media cancán. La pena sería que uno se quedaría más desnudo o más bien, desollado: color fresa, liso, irreconocible.

38)

De las arrugas se dice la verdad a medias, con cuidado. No sea cuestión que nos tomen la palabra y la cuenta de los años y nos volvamos viejos de golpe, como un líquido sobresaturado que se precipita.

39)

Las arrugas son a la vejez lo que el viento es al desierto.

46)

Las arrugas son muy silenciosas. Se ven, pero rara vez se sienten si cerramos los ojos.

47)

Las arrugas se distinguen claramente sobre el cutis, pero no se oyen. No hacen ningún ruido. Aunque pesan mucho: su peso se acumula perfectamente sobre los huesos de la columna hasta doblarla.

48)

Las arrugas que bajan por el cuello parecen goteras.

37)

One would like to pull off half her wrinkles over her head like a wool sweater, and then pull the other half off the feet like nylon tights. The problem would be that one would end up more naked, or else completely emptied, strawberry-colored, smooth, unrecognizable.

38)

We tell the truth about wrinkles slantingly, carefully. We wouldn't want them to take us seriously and suddenly show us all the years that have passed; we wouldn't want to grow old in an instant, like a supersaturated liquid that precipitates.

39)

Wrinkles are to old age what wind is to the desert.

46)

Wrinkles are very silent. They can be seen, but rarely can they be felt if we close our eyes.

47)

Wrinkles stand out clearly on the skin, but they can't be heard. They don't make a single sound. Even though they weigh so much: their weight accumulates perfectly on the backbone until they make it double over.

48)

The wrinkles that descend down the neck look like leaks.

49)

Si consiguiéramos borrarnos una sola arruga borraríamos parte de nuestro nombre.

50)

Si observamos día y noche nuestras incipientes o pequeñas o grandes arrugas, nos acostumbraremos como quien cuida animales de corral. Sólo al final, cuando no podamos más con el gallinero y los conejos, nos daremos cuenta de que nos volvimos viejos.

51)

Vamos sumergidos en el agua de presente: quedan boyando las hebras de las arrugas.

52)

Si una arruga de la frente se levantara como una rígida y blanca espiral, y fuera una idea de pureza, me transformaría en Unicornio.

53)

Una arruga mayor acostumbra ahondar y afirmar su carácter repitiendo un ejercicio hasta el cansancio total del rostro.

54)

En el cuello, las grandes arrugas horizontales forman el imperdible "collar de Venus".

Las mujeres lo llevan a cualquier edad, desprejuiciadamente. Pero con los años, en las cuerditas que bajan del mentón y atan el pescuezo al pecho, cuelgan atrapados alpinistas como lentas arañas que enredaran el collar. Así se origina el temible "nudo en la garganta" donde jadea el viento.

49)

If we could erase even one single wrinkle, we would erase a part of our name.

50)

If we watch by day and by night our incipient or small or big wrinkles, we'll get used to them, like someone taking care of farm animals. Only at the end, when we can't stand that chicken coop, those rabbits any longer, only then will we realize that we have grown old.

51)

We go on, submerged in the waters of the present: the threads of wrinkles keep on floating.

52)

If a wrinkle from the forehead would just stand up like a rigid, white spiral, and if that were a concept of purity, then I would turn into a Unicorn.

53)

A larger-sized wrinkle grows accustomed to deepening and affirming its nature, repeating an exercise until the entire face grows exhausted.

54)

On the neck, the big horizontal wrinkles form the ineluctable "necklace of Venus."
Women wear it at any age, indiscriminately. But as the years go by, trapped mountaineers hang from the little strings that descend from the chin and attach the neck to the chest; they look like slow-moving spiders getting tangled up in the necklace. Thus begins the horrifying "knot in the throat" where the wind keeps panting.

55)

Las arrugas con forma de estrella que nacen en el cuello, señalan el lugar justo donde se juntan los vértices de los dos conos del reloj de arena: la cabeza y el tronco. Es allí por donde pasa toda la arena del tiempo.

56)

Esa apetencia especial que tienen las arrugas u orugas por el rostro, me lleva a pensar que el rostro debe ser tierno como lechuga y fácil como pera madura.

57)

Algunas arrugas de la cara se llevan como si fueran apellidos.

58)

En la claridad del rostro las arrugas van construyendo una enramada cada vez más tupida.

59)

Un ojo como una uva y su correspondiente pata de gallo parada al lado, me dan miedo: creo que el gallo va a picotear la uva.

60)

Un rostro arrugado puede parecer: una hoja de repollo blanco, una hoja de papel crepé castaño oscuro, o un trozo de tela bambula color arena.

61)

Las principales arrugas de la cara son: las "patas de gallo" de los ojos, los "paréntesis" y los "zurcidos" de la boca, los "surcos" de la frente, y los dos "guardias" del entrecejo.

55)

Wrinkles in the shape of a star appear on the neck, signaling the exact place where the vertices from the two halves of the hourglass meet: the head and the trunk. It is through this space that all the sands of time make their passage.

56)

That special way that facial wrinkles or caterpillars have makes me think that the face must be as tender as lettuce and as easy as a ripe pear.

57)

Some facial wrinkles are worn like surnames.

58)

In the face's clarity wrinkles go on building an ever denser canopy.

59)

A grape-like eye and the corresponding crow's foot standing beside it frighten me: I think the crow is about to peck at the grape.

60)

A wrinkled face can look like leaf of white cabbage, a dark, chestnut-colored leaf of crepe paper, or a piece of sand-colored cheesecloth.

61)

The main wrinkles of the face are the "crows' feet" around the eyes, the "parentheses" and "darning" around the mouth," the "furrows" on the forehead and the "guards" between the eyes.

62)

Las arrugas prefieren notoriamente el rostro.

Desde todo nuestro cuerpo la cara se levanta como una flor original entregada a los pacientes depredadores.

Sobre la cara caen inexorables las arrugas y la chupan suave y lento. Se dirían mariposas o caracoles o bichitos de la humedad, y pueden ser ligeras o verdaderas plagas.

Las he visto en el jardín escudiñando en el manzano genealógico, buscando, desesperadas, los rostros delicados.

63)

El rostro propio que uno cree conocer, es un resultado abstracto: la pintura de una flor de Botticelli, de Monet o de Picasso — pudiera ser — que va desapareciendo con disimulo debajo de capas de arrugas o de otras cortinas más sutiles.

No sabemos realmente qué cara es la nuestra ni en qué estación del recuerdo o de lo que deseamos podemos ubicarla.

Un día de primavera, al mirarnos al espejo, vemos que las silenciosas arrugas han cubierto nuestra cara con su delgada piel de musgo, de corcho o de goma plisada.

Y renegamos de todas las escuelas de pintura. Porque no encontramos la flor.

62)

Wrinkles notoriously prefer the face.

From our entire body the face stands up like an original flower given to predatory patients.

On the face wrinkles fall relentlessly and gently, slowly suck it away. You might call them butterflies or snails or pillbugs that come when it's damp. There might be just a few of them, or a full plague.

I've seen them in the garden scrutinizing the genealogical apple tree, desperately searching for delicate faces.

63)

Our own faces that we think we know so well are really an abstraction: a painting of a flower by Botticelli, Monet or Picasso—it could be—that slips away clandestinely behind layers of wrinkles or other more subtle curtains.

We don't really know what face is ours, nor in which season of memory or desire we might place it.

One spring day, while looking in the mirror, we see that the silent wrinkles have covered our own faces with their delicate skin made of moss, cork or pleated rubber.

And we renounce all loyalty to every school of painting. Because we can't find that flower.

de *La botella verde*

from *The Green Bottle* (1995)

translated by Gillian Brassil and Alex Verdolini

La Botella Verde

(Analysis situs)

*Una botella es perfectamente hermosa
además—pregunto—¿tiene interior?

*Como ciertas flores, las botellas
son hermafroditas.

*Una botella guarda lo de adentro y
guarda lo de afuera: superficie
neta, el vidrio corta la realidad en dos: tajada
de dos aguas, linde del mismo mar.

*El día se hace noche ¿cuándo?
Un hombre se hace viejo ¿cuándo?
Una botella vacía, ¿encierra
el espacio que la llena?
El espacio ¿perdona a la botella su
emboscada?
Sutil es el lugar por donde escapa
la vida.

*La botella que habito podría ser
la botella de Klein.
Es decir: toro no orientable.
Botella o toro de alcoholes
topológicos.
Invaginada la realidad dentro del tubo de la
realidad, medito serenamente
sobre el leve error de la transparencia.[1]

---

1   La botella de Klein es un espacio topológico, cuya superficie tiene cualidades sorprendentes: por ej. tiene una sola cara (igual que la Cinta de Möbius), pero siendo una superficie cerrada no tiene interior, como lo tienen la esfera o el toro—también superficies cerradas. Debe su nombre al matemático alemán Félix Klein (1849-1925) que la descubrió en 1871. [AB]

The Green Bottle

(Analysis situs)

*A bottle is perfectly beautiful
does it—I want to know—have an inside also?

*Like certain flowers, bottles
are hermaphrodites.

*A bottle keeps the inside and
the outside: a clean
surface, the glass bisects reality: a slice
through two waters, a border in the same sea.

*At what point does the day become night?
At what point does a man become old?
Does an empty bottle enclose
the space that fills it?
Does the space forgive the bottle for
the ambush?
Life escapes through a fine,
subtle place.

*The bottle I inhabit could be
a Klein bottle.
That is: a non-orientable torus.
A bottle or torus of alcohols,
topological.
Reality sheathed within the tube of
reality, I quietly consider
the slight error of transparency.[1]

---

1   The Klein bottle is a topological space whose surface possesses unusual traits: e.g., it is one-sided (like the Möbius strip) and a closed surface—but unlike other closed surfaces, such as the sphere or the torus, it has no interior. It owes its name to the German mathematician Felix Klein (1849–1925), who discovered it in 1871. *[AB]*

El Sitio

La botella es un cuerpo bello /
objeto oblongo
de la XVIII dinastía egipcia
—siglo XV antes de Cristo—/
o un cuerpo alto y fino
como una "modelo" de TV 1994 /

su color preferido es el verde
hijo del Sr. Silicato de Protóxido de Hierro
y sería un cuerpo completo
pero se ve sin cabeza
y sin extremidades
en esta agresiva posmodernidad
(carencia que casi nadie nota:
sólo algunos pintores y ceramistas
le ponen brazos
y hasta una peqeñísima cabeza
como prótesis equivalentes) /

observen: la botella verde
tiene piel vidriosa / frágil /
transparente /
o es de alguna arcilla satinada
tornasol /

tiene boca chica / redonda / con anillo /
tiene garganta y cuello delicados
por donde desciende la luz
con sus hijos más traviesos: los reflejos /
tiene vientre de venus o de madonna encinta /
tiene culo pequeño / abovedado / misterioso
(el culo de la botella rota / y su cuello partido /
se convierten en gangsters sobre la mesa del bar
o sobre los muros medianeros) /

The Site

The bottle is a beautiful body /
oblong object
from Egypt's eighteenth dynasty
—fifteenth century before Christ—/
or a tall thin body
like a '94 model on TV /

its favorite color is green
son of Sir Silicate of Protoxide of Iron
and it would be a total body
but appears headless
and without extremities
in this aggressive postmodernity
(an absence that nearly nobody perceives:
only a few painters and ceramicists
put arms on it
even a diminutive head,
like prosthetic equivalents) /

observe: the green bottle / its
skin is / vitreous / fragile /
transparent /
or comes from some kind of glossed clay
iridescence /

its mouth is little / round / ringed /
its neck and throat are delicate and
light descends by them
bearing its most mischievous sons: the reflections /
its belly the belly of Venus / or of an expectant madonna /
its bottom small / vaulted / mysterious
(the bottle's broken bottom / and its cleft neck
become thugs on the bar table
or crown the dividing walls) /

tiene dos sexos superpuestos /
uno exterior y otro interior
pene y vagina
a la altura de las costumbres fin de siglo /
además tiene una cavidad húmeda /
central / decisiva /
casa de la posibilidad /
parecida a la imaginación /

no hay duda:
la botella es un cuerpo bello /
habitable /
viviré en su living / en su comedor /
en su cocina /
utilizaré su baño / y su pequeño jardín /
a lo largo de este libro /
y compartiré con Uds. /
mis queridos y cercanos lectores S. XXI /
esta experiencia vital
más común a todos de lo que parece /
porque aquí se encuentran "situados"
("analysis situs")
el hogar y sus límites,
el quehacer y la sofocación
la invención y la angustia
el viento que arranca las hojas afuera
y el oxígeno que exigen los íntimos pulmones /

its sex twofold / superimposed /
an inner and an outer
penis and vagina
after the manner of the fin de siècle /
and there is a damp cavity also /
central / crucial /
house of possibility /
not unlike imagination /

without doubt:
the bottle is a beautiful body /
habitable / I will
take up residence
in its living room / dining
room / kitchen /
use its bath / and its small garden /
over the course of this book /
and will share with you /
dear close readers of the twenty-first century /
this vital experience
more universal than it seems /
because this is the site
("analysis situs")
of the home and its limits,
housework and suffocation
invention and anguish
the wind that tears at the leaves outside
and the oxygen the inner lungs demand /

(la mesa)

se sirvieron de una botella
donde yo no estaba /—nadie lo sabía—/

dentro de otra botella
(también sobre el hule floreado)
mis ojos se daban
despavoridos
contra el vidrio /

(the table)

they used a bottle
where I wasn't /—no one knew—/

within another bottle
(on the floral cloth, also)
my eyes
petrified
bumped up against the glass /

(el guante)

como malla elástica
se ha ajustado la botella
sobre mí /

el vidrio es una membrana transparente:
guante o mucosa continua /
reviste los dedos de la mirada /

desde el interior de la forma
las otras formas / se distancian /
móviles /
externas /
sin adherencias /
casi líquidas /
no sé nada de mí /
apenas algo de lugares /

¿qué de los planos inciertos?
¿ángulos vagos
situados en la brillante telaraña
cazando espacios de mirar?
¿los ojos?
¿qué de la superficie opaca de la muerte?

buho en una cavidad hialina /
así aparezco /
el ave gira en redondo la cabeza /
y mira / y ve / ¿acaso ve lo otro?

la botella me moldea / guante óptico /
verde actual /
elástico hasta ese otro sitio /
¿imposible? ¿peligroso?

me atengo a las consecuencias
y aceptaría la derrota /

(the glove)

like elastic netting
the bottle has shaped itself
around me /

the glass is a clear membrane:
a glove or unbroken film /
sheaths the fingers of vision /

from inside the form
other forms / grow distant /
mobile /
external /
bondless /
nearly liquid /
I know nothing of myself /
nearly nothing of spaces /

what of the vague planes?
uncertain edges
on the shining web
catching spots of sight?
the eyes?
what of death's opaque surface?

an owl in a crystalline cavity /
so I appear /
the bird circles the head
watches / and sees / and sees the other?

the bottle casts me / optic glove
current green /
stretched to that other place /
dangerous? impossible?

I abide by the consequences
and would accept defeat /

(el azul)

cuando se está dentro / como aquí /
no se tiene más que una alta ventanilla
por donde escapar al aire /

brilla el verde artificial /
la luz /
      ¿la misma luz?

afuera ¿qué matiz del invierno?
¿del mismo invierno?

en la ventanilla / no siempre /
canta un pájaro
en diferentes tonos:
azul Picasso / azul Vermeer /
azul Fra Angélico /

(the blue)

when you are inside / as in here /
the only way to free yourself
is through a window, high up /

the artificial green shines /
the light /
    the same light?

outside / which winter shade?
the same winter?

in the window / sometimes /
a bird sings /
in different tones:
blue of Picasso / blue of Vermeer /
blue of Fra Angelico /

(la vitrina)

otra vez / el revés transparente /
ex-libris aéreo /
vitrina del oxígeno /

bebo el discurso cristalino /
y lentamente /
una lente de aumento verde
me rodea /

(the vitrine)

once more / transparent verso /
the ex-libris / aerial /
the oxygen's vitrine /

I drink the crystalline discourse /
and slowly /
a lens of green growth
surrounds me /

(la carta)

escribo una carta infinita
en la pared ambigua
del recipiente que me contiene
unas veces adentro
otras veces afuera
sin levantar el bolígrafo
escribo una carta infinita

(the letter)

I am writing an infinite letter
on the receptacle's uncertain wall
and it contains me
now within
and now without
without lifting the pen
I am writing an infinite letter

(la boa)

cuando Dylan Thomas metió el dedo meñique
dentro del gollete de una inofensiva botella /
y no pudo sacarlo /
llevó su dedo y la botella colgando
a todas partes / sin preocuparse mayormente /

no sabía que él mismo /
había sido atrapado / por el propio
portentoso objeto /

primero fue el dedo / el succionado
por la boca de la botella / luego la mano /
y el brazo / y tras ellos / lento / trabajoso
entró todo el cuerpo /
una verdadera boa constrictor / la botella /

sólo la escritura / el semen alucinante de Dylan
resplandecía / en el proceso de aquella digestión /
a través del estómago vítreo / escamoso /
de la botella /

(the boa)

when Dylan Thomas stuck his pinky finger
into the neck of an unoffending bottle /
and couldn't remove it /
he carried his finger and the dangling bottle
everywhere / largely unconcerned /

he didn't know that he himself /
had been trapped / by that very
portentous form /

his finger was the first / to be sucked
into the mouth of the bottle / then his hand /
and his arm / and then / slow / laborious
his whole body entered /
true boa constrictor / the bottle /

only writing / his hallucinatory semen
shone / over the course of that digestion /
across the glassy / scaly stomach /
of the bottle /

(el puercoespín)

a veces /
algo clausura el espacio que ocupo /
y yo / aquí / me ahogo /

la luz / oscura / atrapada /
se eriza / furioso puercoespín /
y no deja entrar al suave /
elegantísimo / oxígeno /

(the porcupine)

sometimes /
there is a closure in the space I occupy /
and here / I / suffocate /

the light / dark / caught /
it bristles / a porcupine / furious /
and won't let in the smooth /
elegant / oxygen /

(Saturno)

a Rafael Courtoisie

las paredes me rodean de vidriosas posibilidades:
esta silla que me sostiene / se apoya en el eje
central de la botella / gira sobre sí misma:
radar / satélite / anillo de Saturno / ah Cronos /
el viejo Saturno comiéndose a uno de sus hijos /

Goya pudo pintar una instantánea del natural /
me la mostró hace tiempo: monstruosamente
ensangrentados el hijo y la boca del asesino / los
ojos del viejo desorbitados / muy fijos / giran sin
embargo / giran conmigo aquí dentro /

no puedo escaparme de esa idea /

sólo a veces / cuando me subo al jet de mi propia
mirada / y atravieso el vidrio en un viaje
relámpago de ida y vuelta /—como un insecto que
volara veloz desde el interior de su celda hacia
una flor luminosa—/ desciendo / por un instante /
en una estación de afuera /

me engaño /

la calma aparente está acostada en el pasto /

me engaño /

entonces compruebo: / enorme / Saturno el Viejo
ha volado conmigo / me acompaña con su hijo
despedazado / desnudo adolescente a medio comer
(le ha tragado la cabeza y un brazo) / queda el tronco

(Saturn)

for Rafael Courtoisie

the walls surround me with glassy possibilities:
the chair supporting me / pivots on the bottle's
central axis / and orbits itself:
radar / satellite / Saturn's ring / o Kronos /
ancient Saturn eating up one of his sons /

Goya could paint that instant after nature /
he showed me some time ago: monstrously
bloodstained / the son and the murderer's mouth / the
old man's eyes unsocketed / stare / but turn
still / turn in here beside me /

I can't escape that idea /

only at times / when I take the jet of my own
gaze / and cross the glass in a lightning
trip there and back /—like an insect that
will hurtle from its cell out toward
a glowing flower—/ I set down / for an instant /
in an outside station /

I fool myself /

the seeming calm recumbent in the pasture /

I fool myself /

and then I realize: / enormous / Saturn the Ancient
has flown with me / flanks me with his dismembered
son / a naked, half-eaten adolescent
(the head, an arm swallowed) / and what remains is

de un joven del tamaño de las manos del padre /
que lo mantiene por la cintura junto a su boca / la
sangre chorrea y salpica de pintura roja el vidrio
que atravesamos /

el viejo subió al jet de mi mirada / como quien
hubiera encontrado un asiento donde ubicarse / y
viajó conmigo / y vuelve / y entra conmigo hasta la
misma rutinaria silla dentro de esta botella /

the trunk of a boy the size of his father's hands /
held by the waist at his mouth / the
blood drips and peppers with red paint the glass
we are crossing /

the old man boarded the jet of my gaze / like
someone looking for a seat to settle in / and
came with me / and comes back / and comes in with me as far as
the same chair as always in this bottle /

(las hormigas)

cada hormiga arrastra una palabra / su hoja
cortada / enarbolando un velamen oscuro /
la introduce / bandido que se esconde
por el agujero de sílice / desaparecen
los signos / los insectos / el cuello de la botella
traga tela y entraña / hocico de oso hormiguero
la trompa chupa / mientras un eco de vidrio verde
va de cacería / detrás de las trompas horadantes
de Vivaldi /
las hormigas escapan / por las orejas los ojos
la boca de mi cabeza / están allí dentro y las
siento / cada hormiga arrastra un huevo empollado /
la palabra es ahora una larva llena de jugos /
resbalan por la mata de pelo / por la nitidez
de las paredes / su tegumento vivo contrasta
con la arbitrariedad /
el hormiguero disperso / inseguro / entre adentro
y afuera / recibe informes confusos /

(the ants)

each ant drags one word / his piece
of leaf / hoisting a dark sail /
smuggles it / a bandit concealed
through a hole in the silica / they disappear:
the signs / the insects / the bottleneck
swallowing canvas and entrail / anteater snout
the trunk sucks / while an echo of green glass
stalks / behind the horns / boring through /
of Vivaldi /
the ants escape / through the ears the eyes
the mouth, from my head / they are there and
I feel them / each ant drags a hatching egg /
each word a juicy larva /
they slide down my mane / down the spotless
walls / their tegument vivid
against the arbitrariness /
the scattered colony / unstable / between in
and out / takes in crossed signals /

(el telescopio Hubble)

¿dónde la botella primitiva? /
no puedo verla /
¿a qué distancia tengo aquel vidrio verde /
transparente / familiar? /
sigo aquí / concéntrica y excéntrica
en espacios simultáneos /

entrando por el tobogán de mis propias pupilas
descubro botellas sucesivas /
unas dentro de otras / cada vez más íntimas /
más sumisas / más sexuales /
allí "soy muchas" / sub-sumidas
en la más inquietante desnudez /
deslizándose por una orilla interior
del infinito /

en tanto / hacia afuera
la extensión que me separa
de la cobertura exterior /
es insoportablemente inabarcable /

la mirada que sale de mí /
tardaría siglos en recorrer el relámpago /
ese escalofrío salvaje /

el afuera enceguece / y no se ve /
un chorro de galaxias
expanden el recipiente mayor
en desbocada carrera espacial /
los telescopios no lo alcanzan / no llegan /

el Discovery con el Hubble poderoso / partió
en estos días / el gran experto ocular
viaja dentro de una cápsula-botella

(the Hubble telescope)

where is the original bottle? /
I can't see it /
how far do I stand from that green glass /
transparent / familiar? /
I keep on here / concentric and eccentric
in simultaneous spaces /

through the chute of my own pupils /
I discover successive bottles /
bottles within bottles / each time more intimate /
submissive / sexual /
there "I am numerous" / sub-sumed
in the most unsettling nudity /
sliding down the inside edge
of the infinite /

meanwhile / outward
the distance that divides me
from the exterior /
is unbearably unspannable /

it would take /
my sight centuries to trace the bolt /
that savage shiver /

the outside is blinding / and you can't see /
a stream of galaxies
stretching their container, greater,
in an unbridled space race /
the telescopes can't keep up / they don't make it /

the Discovery with the powerful Hubble / took off
in this time / the great ocular expert
travels in a capsule-bottle

que contiene y es contenida / yema
en el huevo / mar en el mar /
ojo en el ojo / su espejo insomne
se multiplica sobre sí mismo /
genético / robótico /

¿son mis propios ojos / naves / límites /
o ratas de laboratorio
en esta trampa donde atrapar el cebo? /

me gustaría quedarme
a esperar los acontecimientos /

pasó el tiempo / hubo inconvenientes /
desperfectos / el Hubble fue reparado
y siguió /

ahora—dijeron—
el Hubble vió los "agujeros negros" /
¿boca enardecida de la botella de Klein?

containing and contained / yolk
within egg / sea within sea /
eye within eye / its insomniac mirror
populates itself /
genetic / robotic /

are my own eyes / ships / limits /
or laboratory rats
in this trap to catch the bait in? /

I would like to stay
and see what happens /

time passed / there were problems /
imperfections / the Hubble was repaired
and kept on /

now—they said—
the Hubble has seen "black holes" /
mouth, inflamed, of a Klein bottle?

(la Fruta)

la botella se muestra: / forma meditando
en el espacio que se vuelve sobre sí mismo /
forma solipsista pero enajenada / superficie
ambigua / sitio de Klein / oxígeno celeste
atrapado en la red pulmonar / espora primigenia /
del lugar del intercambio /

mas / a decir verdad: / la botella parece ser
un lugar estratégico / ilícito / amoral /
suprasexual / de Fruta Prohibida /

veamos: el "Génesis" la ubica en el Paraíso
—nadie creería que allí hubo / alguna vez /
una botella—
sin embargo / el Arbol de Bien y del Mal /
la belleza ofrecida y su condena interior /
enseñan un discurso engañoso /
de botella con "gato encerrado" /

sigamos: el Renacimiento la ilumina:
en el claroscuro de Leonardo / la luz
se apasiona de la sombra / y sin violencia
viola "el cuerpo umbroso" en una habitación
con ventana y boscaje lejano /

el recinto donde ocurre la violación
paracede cerrado / y "el aire deja los extremos
de la sombra en estado confuso"—Leonardo dixit—
confusión de tránsito / y de embotellamiento /

llegamos ahora: la Posmodernidad la colma
de la siniestra Fruta:
a poco del S.XXI / de nuevo
Narciso y su Doble / juntos /abrazados

(the Fruit)

the bottle shows itself: / reflective form
in space that turns upon itself /
a solipsistic form and yet beside itself / uncertain
surface / Klein space / oxygen of heaven
caught in the lung's web / first spore /
of the site of exchange /

yet / in truth: / the bottle seems
a strategic site / illicit / amoral /
suprasexual / Forbidden Fruit /

let us see: Genesis puts it in Paradise
—no one would believe there was once / in that place /
a bottle—
but still / the Tree of Good and Evil /
the beauty offered and the trap within /
teach a deceptive tale /
of a bottle that's off /
a cat / as they say /
locked up in it /

let us continue: the Renaissance illuminates it
in Leonardo's chiaroscuro / the light
thrills for the darkness / and gently
rapes the "umbrous body" in a room
with a window and a distant wood /

the building where the rape occurs appears
locked / and "the air leaves the edges
of the shadow in a blurred state"—thus Leonardo—
blur of traffic / and of bottleneck /

here we are now: Postmodernity brims it up
with the sinister Fruit:

hasta la asfixia / en una agua rígida /
encerrada / rodeados de vidrio verde:
un feto de siameses / en un frasco
de laboratorio /

and at the edge of the twenty-first century / anew
Narcissus and his double / clasped together / verging
on asphyxia / in rigid water /
locked / enclosed in green glass:
a Siamese fetus / in a test
tube /

de *La cuidadora del fuego*

from *The Keeper of the Flame* (2010)

translated by Kristin Dykstra and Kent Johnson

Los culos de El Bosco

Esa obra frontal—los ojos la reciben casi
simultáneamente—¡qué desafío!—
Pero tengo algunas páginas escritas sobre ese
extraño proceso—¿Lo conseguiré?
¿Lo frontal puede hacerse lineal?
Recorrer es una dimensión lineal—
pero en el cuadro impacta la dimensión espacial.

Hojeando el fabuloso libro—empecé a mirar
con cuidadosa morosidad hasta los más
pequeños detalles (tanto como lo permitían
las reproducciones) todos sorprendentes.
Me llamaron la atención insólitas extravagancias,
los culos desnudos—¡y cuánto culo había!
Pensé describirlos uno a uno—
salva sea la parte—
en la medida de mis posibilidades.
Seria esto apenas un sencillo inventario.

¿Los culos están de moda (circa 2005)?
Aunque se trate en general del culo de las mujeres—
mientras en El Bosco son todos culos de hombres.
Para esta parte del cuerpo—trasero—
donde la espalda pierde su honesto nombre—
nombre aplicado a la nalgas de las personas—
o a las ancas de los animales—
en una época (circa 1500) en que la sodomía
era castigado con la muerte—
de estos culos se ocupa el genial pintor flamenco.
¿Qué significan? ¿Creaciones de la libido?
¿Homoerotismo? ¿Autosatisfacción?
¿Lo bello fantástico?
Sobre campo con ojos y bosque con orejas—
los culos desnudos de El Bosco—

The Asses of Bosch

That in-your-face work—the eyes funnel it just about
whole—what provocation!
But I have some notes written on its
weird business—can I manage it?
Can the in-your-face unfold in time?
Roaming is a function of time—
but what overwhelms in the painting is space.

Browsing the baffling book—I began to see,
in measured ways, even the most
minute details (insofar as reproduction
allowed), every one of them a stunner.
Outlandish excesses caught my eye:
the bared asses—and what surfeit of ass to be found there!
I resolved to record them, one by one—
O unspeakable part—
to the best of my limitations.
This then a modest inventory.

Are asses in fashion (circa 2005)?
In custom, one speaks of the woman's ass—
while in Bosch it's the ass of man on display.
Unto this part of the body—the backside
where the back surrenders its honest name—
name given to the human buttocks—
or the rump of beasts—
in an era (circa 1500) when sodomy
meant death—
the brilliant Flemish painter abandons himself to the ass.
What's up with that? Outbursts of the libido?
Medieval queering? Auto-eroticism?
Bizarre beauty?
Over a field with eyes and a forest with ears—
the bared asses of Bosch—

culos con flautas o monedas de oro o golondrinas
culos con ramas, culo con vasija—
culos especiales—el entramado de la libido.
Aquí estos culos no están solos—
la mayoría están enlazados.

Dibujo—culo asomando por una canasta estrecha—
un hombrecito sobre la canasta intenta pegarle
con una mandolina sobre las nalgas desnudas
en el centro de las cuales hay algo
(¿un panal de abejas?).
Dibujo—un culo gordo y sus piernas—
una encogida—la otra de pie con una canasta
de sombrero hasta la cintura y una lanza
que atraviesa un costado de la barriga
y un costado de la cara.
Óleo—círculo abajo a la izquierda—martillando
sobre un culo desnudo—un culo que echa humo.
¿Y otros?
Óleo sobre tabla—El infierno—culo
más piernas entre alas.
Culo atravesado por una rama fina.

Culo ensartado con corneta larga y piernas.
Culo y una pierna encogidos bajo un sombrero
o un molusco que cubre la parte superior
del cuerpo hasta la cintura. Por el culo
entra una lanza y sale por la punta
del molusco o sombrero.
Culo y piernas en una vasija.
Culo y piernas con una vara ensartada
empujada por un mono.
Culo ¿con cola de mono?

Óleo—culo con piernas hincadas
saliendo de bajo una cortina.

asses with sticks, ass with anaphora—
special asses—the core of the libido.
Here, asses are not autonomous—
most of them are entangled.

Sketch—ass peeking from narrow basket,
a little man bent over the basket whacks at it
with mandolin—
there's something lodged between the buttocks
(honeycomb of bees?)
Sketch—fat ass and legs—
one tucked up—the other standing in a hat basket
up to waist and with spear
run-through from stomach's side and
out the face.
Oil—circle of figures bottom left—whacking
bared ass—ass spewing steam.
And more?
Oil on panel—Hell—ass
plus legs with wings.
Ass with fine branch shoved in.

Ass penetrated by long cornet and legs.
Ass and leg huddled under hat
or mollusk covering upper section of body
to waist. Into the ass
goes a lance, emerging from the top
of the mollusk or hat.
Ass and legs in a vessel.
Ass and legs skewered with pole,
pushed along by an ape.
Monkey-tailed ass?

Oil—ass with kneeling legs,
beneath raised arras.
Little ass of child?

Culito de niño?
Dibujo—culos con sus piernas empujan
un eje con dos círculos—ruedas.
Culo y piernas con calzas y sombrero
hongo hasta la cintura—
cabeza de pez y brazos.

Óleo—culo con flauta clavada.
Culo subiendo escalera, con dardo.
Culo con pica clavada.

Óleo—culo de mujer desnuda—
de donde salen flores.
Conjunto de culos y de piernas circulan
de rodillas con las cabezas hacia el centro
(que no se ven)—sobre cada culo un pajarraco negro.

Culo que asoma entre dos valvas gigantes
que lleva al hombro una mujer desnuda.
Culo con la cola llena de las espinas
de una frutilla roja gigante—terminada
en una flor con puntos verdeazul.
Tres culos celestes con las piernas en el aire—
los cuerpos no se ven porque están dentro
de una gran caparazón rojiza
que termina en cola de alacrán.
Un conjunto de hombres desnudos la sostienen
y la empujan—encima un oso
y sobre el oso un parajito verde.

Óleo—monstruo con cabeza de pájaro.
Culo que arroja monedas de oro.
Culo con gran espejo convexo y ovalado
donde se reflejan la cara de una mujer
y una de lobo al costado.
El cuerpo está de rodillas

Sketch—asses with legs push
an axle with two circles—wheels.
Ass and legs with breeches and hat,
a toadstool to waist—
fish head and arms.

Oil—ass pricked with flute.
Ass climbing ladder, with banderilla.
Ass penetrated with pike.

Oil—O, a naked woman's ass—
from which flowers come.
Conclave of asses and legs circumnavigate
on knees, heads facing in
(not seen)—a great dark bird alighted on every ass.

Ass peeking out between two giant valves,
nude woman riding its shoulder.
Ass stuck with spines
of a giant red berry—the ass
becoming flower, turquoise spotted.
Three sky-blue asses, legs akimbo—
the torsos not seen; they're inside
a great reddish carapace,
which waves a scorpion tail.
A cluster of naked men shoulder it forth,
push it forward—a bear on top,
and atop the bear a little green bird.

Oil—beast with bird head.
Ass that fountains coins of gold.
Ass with big oval mirror, convex,
where the face of a woman is reflected
and that of wolf, too.
The body is on its knees,
cloaked in a cloth.

tapado por una tela.
Las piernas de ese culo terminan en ramas
de árbol secas que abrazan a la mujer.
Culo con flauta incrustada.
Culo hacia arriba de un cuerpo desnudo horizontal—
la cabeza y los brazos están dentro del pico
de un gran pajarraco—la cabeza
tiene de sombrero una marmita.
Un brazo de esta criatura sostiene
el culo y las piernas—del culo sale
una bandada de golondrinas negras.

Óleo—Tentación de San Antonio—
parte trasera (culo) de un animal
con las patas calzadas de botas.
La cabeza es de mujer tocada de plumas
y pelos fumando—o tocando una gaita—
mira de frente—en la cola fina levantada
está parado un pájaro—especie de lechuza—
bajo la cola surge un chorro líquido.

Culo con piernas hincadas de las que salen
ramitas—el cuerpo no se ve—está cubierto
con una capa fina de tela verdosa—
sale la cabeza de perfil
con una flecha clavada en la frente.
En el cielo un barco—y el culo de un hombre
desnudo muestra la cabeza entre las piernas.

Óleo—el culo redondo grande de una vasija
de barro—la cola forma el asa de la vasija—
palos metidos en el culo—
de la boca de la vasija cae un chorro de agua.

Óleo—un culo y piernas de hombre negro—
peludo—con una rama gruesa bifurcada

The legs of that ass become branches,
parched, entwining woman.
Ass with flute protruding
ass in the air from prone body—
head and arms inside beak
of great bird—the head
wears a pot for hat.
An arm of the creature holds up
the ass and legs—a flock of black swallows
flies out the ass.

Oil—Temptation of Saint Anthony—
back part (ass) of an animal,
feet in boots.
The head is a woman's, feathered,
she smokes—or blows on bagpipe—
she stares straight ahead—on her upraised tail
a bird is perched—a manner of owl—
beneath whose tail a liquid shoots.

Ass on squatting legs from which
small branches bud—the body is hidden—covered
with hood of rich greenish cloth—
the head pokes out in silhouette,
arrow buried in its brow.
Boat in the sky—naked man's ass,
head looking back between thighs.

Oil—fat round ass from mud
vessel—its tail curves to make the handle—
sticks shoved up the ass—
from the rim of the vessel water is pouring.

Oil—ass and limbs of a Black man—
hairy, him—with thick forked branch,
thorn-covered, shoved in the anus—body

espinosa incrustada en el ano—el cuerpo
cubierto de una rosa blanca.
Unas piernas negras llevan zapatos blancos.
Una espada blanca atraviesa el muslo.
Sobre ramas fijas en el ano
está posada una garza pelada
con cola de pavo real de un color claro—
casi transparente.
En una nervadura de esa rama blanca
hay atada una cuerda que tira de un barquito anaranjado
donde navega una cabeza de mono
con manos como garras en la cabeza.

¡Culo veo, culo quiero!
¡Atar esas moscas por el rabo!
Articulación de artículo—es
arte con culo.

covered by a white rose.
Black legs wear white shoes.
White sword run through thigh.
On fixed branches in anus
a featherless egret stands
with peacock's tail, a flesh color—
almost transparent.
To a crotch of white branch
a rope is fastened, pulling little orange boat
sailed by ape's head,
claw hands digging into little head.

Ass I see, ass I covet!
Tie those flies up by their snaky tails!
Articulation of the articulo—it's
Art with ass.

[KJ]

Amorino

Cáncer, signo de agua. El aguamadre de los alquimistas.
El agua de la vida. En el planeta Marte se está buscando
agua. Sin agua no hay vida. Partió una sonda
en estos días para allá. El cangrejo vive en el agua
y en la tierra—y camina de costado. Yo tengo
un *"Amorino que cavalca un granchio"* (cangrejo).
Lo traje de Pompeya. Me gustaría que estuviera
en la carátula de mis Obras Completas.

Amorino

Cancer, a water sign. Motherwater of the alchemists.
Water of life. They're searching for water on planet
Mars. Without water there is no life. Recently a probe
set out for Mars. The crab lives in water
and on land—and the crab walks sideways. I have
an *Amorino que cavalca un granchio* (Cupid riding a crab).
I brought it back from Pompeii. I'd like it to appear
on the cover of my Complete Works.

[KD]

Leonardo da Vinci y yo

Cuando tenía trece, catorce años
yo quería ser como Leonardo da Vinci.
Leí una biografía de Leonardo: *La resurrección
de los dioses* creo que se llamaba (me la regaló
mi madre), por Dmitri Merejkovski, el marido
de Zinaida Gippius, poeta rusa de la Edad de Plata.
Me deslumbró Leonardo. Yo quería ser como él.
El era zurdo—yo era zurda—él era inventor—
yo quería pintar—él, la geometría—yo, la geometría—
él, en vuelo—yo soñaba que volaba—él escribía
sus manuscritos con la mano izquierda, yendo de derecha
a izquierda—y se leían a derechas reflejados en un espejo—
eran secretos. Yo escribí y saqué apuntes y escribí
muchas cosas de esa manera. Él era el maestro—yo
la discípula. Había pegado con chinches muchos dibujos
de Leonardo: cabezas, caras fascinantes en la pared de mi
cuarto—también mantos—guindo oscuro y verde musgo
de los paisajes lejanos—que me absorbían la vista
cuando miraba las reproducciones de sus misteriosas pinturas.
Él inventaba alas—yo imaginaba un mecanismo
de espejos sobre una esfera que recibiera a luz del sol
en forma sucesiva para iluminar y calentar el Polo Norte.
En esa época no le daba importancia al Polo Sur.
Tampoco podía imaginar qué pasaría si se derretían ambos polos.
Por ahí deben estar los dibujos—hechos a compás.
Ya sé que los rusos hace unos meses enviaron un gran espejo
desplegable como un paraguas a la estratosfera—
con propósito parecido. Pero fracasó. El espejo no se abrió.
Con Leonardo era diferente. Las matemáticas,
la geometría, el vuelo, la sombra, el claroscuro,
la penumbra, la sonrisa insinuada, el color como seducción
—mucho después me encontré con todo eso—en los museos
sentí de golpe el palpitar del corazón de Leonardo.
A la Gioconda le pusieron bigotes—o la hicieron bizca—

Leonardo da Vinci and Me

When I was thirteen, fourteen years old,
I wanted to be like Leonardo da Vinci.
I read a biography of Leonardo: *Resurrection
of the Gods*, I think it was called (gift from
my mother), by Dmitri Merejkovski, the husband
of Zinaida Gippius, Russian poet of the Silver Age.
Leonardo dazzled me. I yearned to be like him.
He was a southpaw; I was a southpaw. He was an inventor;
I longed to paint—geometry his; geometry mine—
he in flight; I dreamt I flew—he wrote his manuscripts
with left hand, moving right to left—and mirrored, they read aright—
encrypted. I wrote and took notes and wrote
lots of things in that direction. He was the master, I
the disciple. I'd tacked up lots of Leonardo's
drawings: heads, magnificent faces, on the walls
of my room—also the robes—dark and moss-green
like the far lands—my gaze fixed
in the strange reproductions.
He'd dream up wings—I thought up a device
of mirrors above a sphere, reflecting the sun
in repeating waves to illumine and heat-up the North Pole.
Back then, Antarctica wasn't much on my mind.
Nor was I aware, alas, what would happen if the poles did melt.
The plan should be somewhere, compass-made.
I know the Russians sent up a great mirror a few months back,
one that unfolds umbrella-like in the stratosphere
with like purpose. But it flopped. The mirror would not unfold.
With Leonardo things weren't like that. Mathematics,
geometry, flight, shadow, chiaroscuro,
penumbra, the sly smile, color as erotic
—much later I discovered all that—in the museums
I felt his heartbeat inside me!
They put a mustache on Gioconda—or turned her cross-eyed
—they gave her hand a Parkinson's flutter

movieron su mano como si tuviera Parkinson—
pero la Gioconda sonríe leve—tanto que a veces
no lo parece. La Gioconda es sobrenatural.
Habita el tiempo. Su propia casa.

—but Gioconda keeps smiling, faintly—so faintly it almost seems she isn't. Gioconda is freaky.
She inhabits time. It is her very house.

[KJ]

La tortilla

Escribo esto que recuerdo de hace mucho:
La tortilla de papas gigante, del tamaño de la habitación,
como un platillo volador, girando sobre mi cabeza.
Yo estaba enferma en cama con mucha fiebre
y me habían dado un opiáceo como calmante.
Y la tortilla a manchas blancas y amarillas
(papa y huevo)—gruesa—giraba y giraba.
Bajaba hasta el borde de mi cabeza—y subía girando.
Yo tendría diez u once años. Me persiguió toda la tarde.

Spanish Tortilla

This memory I'm recording is from long ago:
A colossal potato tortilla the size of my room
rotates over my head like a flying saucer.
I was sick in bed with a high fever
and they gave me opiates for the pain.
Speckled white and yellow (potato and egg),
the tortilla—a fat one—spun around and around.
It descended to the top of my head—and rose, spinning.
I must have been ten or eleven. That tortilla trailed me all afternoon.

[KD]

El pantum .

Un querido recuerdo:
"Tu carne de lunas morenas
celebra litúrgicos himnos frutales".
Creo que era en forma de pantum.
Sí lo era. Estoy segura.
Y era cadencioso, como el oleaje del mar
en la orilla y era creciente
y era de día—y era nocturno. Iba y volvía
como una intensa ola de amor.

The Pantoum

A cherished memory:
"Your flesh of dark moons
hosannas the liturgical hymns of the orchards."
I think it was in a pantoum.
Yes, it was. I'm sure of it.
And it was insistent, like the lapping
on the shore, and it grew
and it was of day—and it was of night. It retreated and returned
like an intense wave of love.

[K J]

Imago mundi

Qué difícil—esa infinita modulación de la luz—centella
y reflejo—brillos—destellos—biombo de espejos—
hoguera con sombra abismada detrás de las llamas—
cuando el revés de lo oscuro es todo luz—y esa imagen—
un pulpo de plata ardiente—enciende la mirada que construye
el monstruo—el múltiple tentáculo de la desbordada
apariencia. El mundo—nuestro mundo.

Imago Mundi

So hard to capture—that infinite modulation of light—spark
and reflection gleams—glints—screen comprised of mirrors—
bonfire with shadow plunging behind flame—
when the flip side of dark is total light—and that image—
an octopus in fiery silver—ignites the gaze that structures
the monster—the manifold tentacle of appearance
spilled over. The world—our world.

[KD]

Encuentro extramuros con Isidoro Ducasse

I

Encontrarnos a orillas del mar
sobre un peñasco de la costa—fue la cita.
Él—evanescente pez metafórico—
perverso y ágil—
tocándome apenas la punta de los dedos
con sus aletas—su vientre de piel azul
con un ojo de sangre—su mirada
de medusa escarlata—

me dijo: No vuelvas la cabeza que morirás—
quédate alga o musgo en el hueco
de la roca—
te protegerán guijarros—pezuñas de dolor.

Se levantó ante mí—sentí que se enderezaba
el océano—y me tragué la realidad—
mientras oía la caída de un meteoro
sobre Montevideo.
Sin embargo—Isidoro Ducasse—
era un niño transparente—sentado
a mi lado.

Lo tomé en mis brazos
y lo amamanté de certeza material—
hasta que lo entregué de nuevo al mar.

Encounter with Isidore Ducasse Outside City Walls

I

Meeting by the sea
on a coastal crag—was the plan.
He—evanescent metaphorical fish—
perverse and agile—
lightly grazing my fingertips
with his fins—his blue-skinned belly
and bloody eye—his
scarlet medusa sight—

he said: Don't turn to look or you're dead—
stay here, be algae or moss inside a hole
in the rock—
pebbles will protect you—sorrow hooves.

It rose against me—I felt the ocean
right itself —and I drank reality down—
hearing a meteor fall
across Montevideo.
Still—Isidore Ducasse—
was a boy, transparent—sitting
beside me.

I took him in my arms
and suckled him with material certainty—
then released him back to the sea.

II

Où s'en vont ils, de ce galop insensé?

Ibas a caballo al galope sobre la orilla arenosa—
a vuelo de pájaro te observaba
desde un helicóptero—
modelo fin del siglo XX.
La espuma del Río de la Plata
caía sobre las huellas de los cascos veloces—
y tú crecías—Maldoror—jinete mutante
del Apocalipsis.

III

La noción de la divinidad
está centrada en la realidad eficiente
aunque sobrehumana—cuyo misterio satisface
a las tinieblas y al infinito.
No hay blasfemo ni réprobo—hay poesía—
palabra escrita—en presente
atravesando el tiempo.

II

Où s'en vont ils, de ce galop insensé?

You were galloping on horseback across the sandy shore—
I had a birdseye view
from a helicopter—
a late 20th century model.
Lather from the Río de la Plata
fell in the tracks left by quickfire hooves—
and you were increasing in size—Maldoror—mutant horseman
of the Apocalypse.

III

The notion of the divine
centers on a reality that is efficient
yet superhuman—whose mystery satisfies
darkness and infinitude.
There's neither blasphemy nor condemnation—there is poetry—
word written—in the present
traveling across time.

[KD]

El derrumbamiento

Ha ocurrido un derrumbamiento—
mezcla de lodo y amargas burbujas
las circunstancias conjugan
el bajo aplomo de la miseria humana—
lento deslizamiento hacia la nada—
el reloj se apura—está como loco—da vueltas
por los entretelones
y grita y grita y nadie escucha—
nadie clama—o llora—estamos trabados
en los engranajes de nervio y sangre.
La potente sombra arrastra como torrente
hacia la nada—esa poderosa—callada—
demencial secuencia que llevamos puesta
al despojado esqueleto—o jaula—
o trampa—para encerrar el sigiloso destino—
o intestino abierto—o cielo repetido—
hasta clausurar las puertas.

Implosion

Implosion—
stew of mud and bitter froth
fate conjugates
the lower case of human folly—
slow slide towards oblivion—
the clock—goes wild—spins tic-toc
under muffling veils
tolls-tolls to no avail—
no one clamors—or wails—we're stuck
in gears of nerve and vein.
The great shadow floods and drags
towards the no-subject—regal—hushed—
preposterous sequence enshrouding
the skeletal core—or cell—
or trap—to cage furtive destiny—
or the glowing bowels—or the repeating sky—
until all doors go cancelled.

[KJ]

Casi sobrenatural

Se me vino encima toda la Constelación del Navío—luces—
brillos de extraña magnitud—agujeros de sombra—infinita
oscuridad salida de madre en medio de un temporal concierto
casi insufrible. Bajemos a la realidad—¿la realidad cuál?
¿las palabras? ¿los libros? Estoy aquí—sola—escrutando.
El sauce cae sobre la ventana—que me mira—y llueve dulcemente—
es mediodía—y la luz afuera es poca—tamizada
de verdes entre las largas ramas que cuelgan—detenidas—
y sobre la mesa—dos rosas rojas alicaídas en un vaso—dos
jazmines boqueando angustia—¡sálvame! ¡sálvame!—
palabra—hija de dioses que desconozco. Sigue
mi destino sosteniendo el cielo abierto—constelado—
donde viaja sin descanso—sereno y encendido—el Navío—
siempre presente—desmedido—casi sobrenatural—tiempo
vivo—mi tiempo—nuestro tiempo—nuestra palabra testigo—
nuestro pulso que cuenta los segundos—a veces—
como si fueran siglos—y otras veces
cesa definitivamente—¿definitivamente?
¿Y yo dónde estoy? Lo miro—lo repaso—¡es tan hermoso!
con su carátula nocturna—honda—donde pasa
el Navío y sus estrellas de primera magnitud—
y estoy en tierra—en mi casa—aquí sobre la mesa
escribiendo—esta línea larga de escritura
que apenas me da cierta certeza. Creo que estoy viva—
quizá—por eso—digo esto. ¿Y el libro qué dice?
Está afuera, no hay duda—estacionado—en un borde.
Soy amiga del Infinito—le pido que lo lleve con él.
Estoy entre los frutos colmados del verano—
con el ananá querido y la sandía sangrienta
entre las manos—y el durazno de terciopelo
como los fabulosos príncipes de la niñez
y las uvas en copiosos racimos—desbordando
esta contradictoria—injusta—anómala frutera terrestre—
aquí en este comedor—jardín—espejo de mi cara—
y deslumbrada voy—como un cáliz de sombra
que se abriera al alba y alcanzara a dar flor.

Practically Supernatural

The entire Argo Navis constellation settled over me—lights—
gleams of weird magnitude—holes black with shadow—infinite
darkness spilled from mother into an almost intolerable
concert of squalls. Let's drop back to reality—what reality?
Words? Books? I'm here—alone—recounting.
Willow falls across the window—looking at me—and rain falls sweetly—
at noon—and there's little light outside—sifted
through greens from low-hanging branches—as they pause—
and on the table—two red roses drooping in a glass—two
jasmine flowers gasping in anguish—rescue me! rescue me!—
word—daughter of gods unknown to me. It tracks my fate
holding up the open sky—full of stars—
where it travels without pause—serene and burning bright—the Ship—
always there—supernatural?—out of proportion—deep
time—my time—our time—our word as witness—
our pulse counting seconds—sometimes—
as though they were centuries—and sometimes
it stops definitively—definitively?
And where am I? I look at it—go over it—so beautiful!
with its nocturnal mask—its sounding depths—where the Ship
and its first-magnitude stars move past—
and I'm on earth—in my house—here writing at the
table—this long line of words
that delivers little certainty. I think I'm alive—
maybe?—and so—I say this. What does the book say?
It's outside, no doubt about it—parked—on a borderline.
I'm friend to the Infinite—I ask him to take the book.
Summer's abundant fruits are all around me—
dear pineapple and blood-red watermelon
in my hands—and velvety peach
like the fabled princes from my childhood
and grapes on copious vines—spilling over
this contradictory—unjust—anomalous terrestrial bowl—
here in this dining room—garden—mirror of my face—
and I am dazed—like a chalice of shadows
that may open to the dawn, and into blossom.

[KD]

A partir de Emily Dickinson

Nuestra jornada había avanzado—
Nuestros pies habían casi llegado
A la singular bifurcación en la Ruta del Ser—
La Eternidad—por Término.—

Nuestros pasos de pronto sintieron miedo—
Nuestros pies—reacios—nos llevaban—
Delante—estaban las ciudades—pero en medio—
La floresta de la Muerte—

Retroceder—era imposible—
Detrás—una Ruta Sellada—
La Bandera Blanca de la Eternidad—delante—
Y Dios—en todas las Puertas.

After Emily Dickinson

Our journey arrived this far—
Our feet almost touched
The split of Being's route—
Eternity—branching End.

Our steps sensed a rushing fear—
Our pace—stubborn—took us—
Forward—there were cities—but flowering midst—
The anthology of Death—

To return—impossible—
Behind—a Sealed Path—
The White Flag of Always—in front—
And God—in every Door.

[KJ]

INTERVIEW: The Table, A Mad Dance of Electrons
Silvia Guerra interviews Amanda Berenguer

Translation by Jeannine Marie Pitas

How did your first relationship with poetry come about?

I've been asked that question various times, and my answer is always more or less the same. My relationship with poetry began in school, when we all had to write the notorious "composition." The first one I wrote was entitled "The Palm Tree," and it was set in the desert. I remember writing "The Palm Tree" as the title and underneath it the word "Composition." This made the word "composition" look like a lizard at the foot of the palm tree. I guess this was because the word "composition" was long, and to me it looked like a lizard in the sand.

Another unforgettable thing that led me to write was one time when I turned a corner and saw a dead dog at the side of the road. That dead dog, swollen with a little thread of dirty water running out of him... People were passing by and no one else took any notice, but I experienced a kind of fall into nothingness. Something opened up in me, a feeling that I came to know again and again, many times over. Afterwards I went home and wrote something about that sensation I had just experienced.

Why did I feel the need to write that? I really can't say.

Another occasion—also having to do with death—was when I saw one of my deceased aunts in her closed casket. Since she had died of tuberculosis, they closed the casket in order to prevent contamination. It was a type of casket with a transparent crystal diamond cut into the cover, revealing her face. I must have been about fourteen years old, and I'd never seen a dead body before. I remember leaning over and seeing my aunt's face; even now my hair stands on end at the memory. But it's not just an emotion. It's more the sense of an abyss, of another dimension.

A tremendously deep well.

You have stated: "My biography is a succession of linguistic events. That's all I have." Does language come before everything else?

I think so. The word and all its resonances. I think that in order to understand what I mean here, one would need immediately to imagine a world without words. Without intelligent communication, without simple communication. It is by means of words that I lead my life.

"In the beginning was the word." The writers of that statement were well aware of its truth.

Which books do you always go back to?

There's a fundamental book that I adore, and I say the same thing to all the poets who at one point or another ask me this question: the dictionary. You have to know how to read the dictionary. It's a fascinating book. Due to the many meanings of the words as well as the act of searching for those words within their pages. Of course I read dictionaries a lot, since they have to do with language. They contain an entire world, the universe expressed in words. Indeed, the entire universe is encased within a dictionary; not one thing escapes. It isn't that the words are linked together in a certain order; each one is separate yet joined to the others, and each word is a world. When you read the word "chair," a chair is created. When you read the word "universe," what other thing can be greater than the meaning of the word "universe?" The words grant you an entrance into the meanings. Everything is contained therein; nothing escapes. Only silences.

You are focused on a concept of language as suggested by the saying, "Language is the divining rod that discovers wells of thought."

 Each word causes you to enter a different sphere. But this sphere isn't a well. A well is something you fall into—there's no falling here. No, the word draws you into its sphere and creates an area that might be a well, but it's also a very full, large, and luminous space. Through the word we enter another dimension.

Is writing an effort for you?

No, no. It's a necessity.

On the contrary, writing excites me. Sure, of course there are some days when you feel empty inside, but that's different. That feeling is the other side of the coin. Sometimes a flower, or a sound, or a dream, a sensation, a word, a phrase, a cloud—this is enough to get me started.

Is poetry a perception of reality?

One might say it is. Poetry is perception, sensation, imagination. It has everything to do with the world and the self. And it's all completely inside our mind, not on the outside. So then, where is reality? Inside or outside?

How do you define poetry?

It's another dimension that you enter by way of words, music, painting, color. Poetry goes beyond the mere written word. When I speak of the wonder of this world, I am speaking of everything. Poetry can exist on every plane.

Do you consider poetry to hold something of the sacred?

No, poetry is not in the realm of the sacred. There is something superior about it, but "superior" is not the right word either. The word "sacred" is not easy to define. My opinion is that poetry is an extraordinary realm where you can experience a different dimension. Poetry makes you see the world in a different way, and I don't know if that dimension is sacred or not. I don't know. At times one gets confused by the word "sacred," and I myself am not acquainted with any gods.

You don't have a God?

I don't.

So, what idea do you have of paradise?

Paradise is on earth. I believe that life is amazing.

I suppose that a paradise should be a marvelous place, and I think that life contains some marvelous moments. It might be a sunset, a conversation. I don't know, every time I think about the great quantity of things that exist, these roses for instance, you might say that in them I see the wonder of life. It's not paradise; the word "paradise" sounds artificial to me, too much in the realm of a specific thing, a determined place. No, no, paradise is here.

At times there's really very little paradise present, and suddenly you find yourself in other regions. You might pass through a space of nothingness, you might get stuck in the mud. But there are still moments in life when...

Would you say that language can change the world?

Change it? That's a tall order. To a certain extent language modifies the world because if everything changes, then you realize that certain changes are bound to occur. But I don't know, when you say "change the world," I think you are talking about making some kind of lasting, substantial difference. But the world is always changing, and it's always the same.

Tell me about the construction of an image and a poetic "I" in relation to places and objects.

Ah! I have a very strange relationship with both objects and places.

The image fundamentally depends on where you place the object, and also where you place yourself. It happened to occur to me to place myself inside a bottle, and to feel that I'm inside a bottle. *The Green Bottle* is just that: a place without a place.

This occurs with the Möbius strip because it's a surface that has neither inside nor outside. Or with the Klein bottle, where you have to invaginate part of the neck inside its own shape, and you can't do it. You know it's an illusion or something, because with the Möbius strip, you can twist it a certain way and you see the surface, but with the Klein bottle you don't. I spent several days trying to build one, and I know that some sculptors have done it. It can also be made as a hologram, right?

It's just amazing, the way you go on discovering things little by little throughout life, because everything you're looking for is right there in front of you.

So, why do you go discovering things in little bits? It might be due to the changes that occur—when you look at things in a different way, it seems that you are seeing them for the first time.

What can you tell me about image and metaphor?

To me, a metaphor seems to be a surprising journey that is always possible. What's extraordinary about metaphors is their ability to connect distances, to relate images instantly like a ray of light without any space in between. It's incredibly strange. You jump from one place to another and this puts you in another region, another world that I find fascinating.

A metaphor is called by that name for a reason; it is a leap toward the beyond, and of course it carries you to the other side, to other regions, other places.

Do you think that there is a strong connection between the intimate world of your home and the reverberation of a whale like "a luminous tear?"

I feel that I'm transparent and the world comes into my house, and also that I go out to meet it. I don't have the feeling of being inside a house. I have the feeling of being in the world. This might sound very pretentious, but I feel that I'm in a place where things are kind to me, and it's such a beautiful place. I'm always talking about this other dimension. It's very hard to characterize it. I don't know if it's the fourth dimension, but then, at times I think *this* world, *this* moment is actually that other space. Sometimes I feel that everything that surrounds us, the things, the beings, the words, that at times are for me like objects, the sayings, the flowers, what we eat, what we touch, everything. I'd say that everything forms part of a magical world.

I believe that we live in a kind of enchanted madness.

Is it the meaning of language that leads you to poetry?

Yes, it might be. Poetry has a soul, a body; in itself it is a kind of power. Poetry is power. It defends itself. It has defended itself again and again. Poetry always defends itself. It saves itself.

So, would you say that the experience of language is what drives you to write?

I am driven to write by something I don't know.

Deep down I don't know why I write. The need for expression more than the need to express myself. I feel that "to express oneself" means something other than stepping outside of oneself.

For this reason we need contact with the other that sometimes occurs and sometimes does not occur. I don't know what the phrase "to express" means exactly, but the "ex" makes me think that it has something to do with an exit, with stepping out or leaving, and the "press" makes me think of imprisonment. So, expression has to do with escaping from a sort of prison.

And what about your muse?

It seems a little ironic, a little funny, but I don't take the word "muse" all that seriously. It sounds like inspiration, perhaps a gift of some sort... I don't know. Sometimes you write without really understanding what you're writing, and at other times there are different factors that lead to writing. You don't really know just who is murmuring in your ear, who is speaking to you.

Is it the "voice of language?"

It seems to be language itself. Sometimes language presents you with a little phrase that wakes you up in the night.

Sometimes I might randomly think of a word, and then I turn on the radio and right in that moment they're saying that same word. It must be sheer coincidence, right? The same word, or the same sound. And you might forget about it later... but not always, eh? In this last poem that I wrote *(The Table of the Third Millennium)* there are selections in prose, but I'm sure that if you read and examine them carefully, even the prose, the spots with periods and commas, have a certain rhythm, something that isn't quite what normally comes to mind when we think of prose. This is why, when I finish a poem, I need to read it aloud.

Does a completed text set a precedent for a later one?

This can happen when dealing with rough drafts. Sometimes, there are pieces of text right within your own writing; this is why I so very much like to keep a notebook. For me the notebook is filled with interchangeable papers; you can write something and leave it because you know that it's a seed that will germinate later on. You know that it is a mode of speech or a shape that you found in this particular moment, and later it might be derived or transformed into something else that interests you as well. This is how I always explain my way of working. While writing a draft, I also write on the edges, in the margins. I might add a half dozen words, four or five images that could potentially be substituted or inserted into the main piece. So, I leave my drafts annotated, and at the same time a little branch comes out. I always say that there is something horticultural about writing; it grows branches and little roots.

This growth has to do with diction, which itself refers to oral speech. In the recording I made, which is entitled *Dictions*, I proposed something very particular.[1] I decided to record myself on four tracks that I then superimposed; this allowed an almost symphonic sound that I found very exciting. And in a given moment I decided to listen to these texts—they were then already recorded—to hear the sounds of the words, the low tones, the sharp ones, the rises and falls, the depths and luminosities. It always seemed to me that the high tones had to be sharp, the low ones needed to be deep. So this is completely arbitrary, but it's my general notion. Some letters seems sharp to me—and I believe that in fact they are. Others are low. And so, without any kind of music, simply grounding myself in the intention of the word, so to speak—lengthening it, stretching it, turning it on its head—I created this "diction."

What would you say about musicality in relation to rhythm and rhyme?

Well, this is part of everything we've been saying. In my first period as a writer, the time of my enthusiasm with Mallarmé and Valéry—especially Valéry —I began to get a sense of that elaborately fashioned verse with its perfect rhyme. I love *The Marine Cemetery*, and when Valéry passed away in 1945, I wrote an "Elegy on the Death of Paul Valéry" because I was so crazily enthusiastic about him. And what did I do before anything else? I tried to discover a different kind of stanza that would have some different characteristics than the usual. A totally new kind of stanza. Now, I feel that what I produced was a little old-fashioned, but what occurred to me then was a

---

1 The recording, entitled *Dicciones* in the Spanish, first appeared in 1973.

highly complicated strophe. I don't know if it had rhyming couplets or alternating hendecasyllabic rhymes —I can't remember it well enough—but I'm pretty sure that it had nothing to do with any aspect of Valéry's poetry.

I also experimented with many other things; I have everything from vidalitas to other types of song.[2] The book dedicated to my mother is entitled *Countersong*; many of those poems were sung and, well, they are adapted to become shorter verses with their rhymes, but not always—sometimes there are loads of internal rhymes.

Sometimes it happens that one word leads me to another, and the other attracts me due to its musicality.

What music do you listen to?

I have listened to the music that we've all listened to, the great classical pieces—Stravinsky, Beethoven, Vivaldi. I also like that more primitive music that comes from the bottom up, from the earth. I'm really drawn to those forms. And, I like the Beatles. I don't enjoy much rock music; in general I don't like the lyrics. But, something special happened to me with the Beatles. I adore them.

What about tango?

Gardel, and also the dance. The rhythm of tango. The relationship between the man and the woman, that thing that moves from sensuality to sexuality within the rhythm itself.

And Gardel, his voice, his way of singing. It's one of a kind.

That intonation: no sound is the same as any other. He doesn't repeat himself; it's as if he were always singing for the first time.

---

2 *Vidalitas* are folkloric songs that are typical of the northwest regions of Argentina and were popularized in Uruguay in the late nineteenth century.

Can one arrive at poetry from different places?

Ah, I believe so. Not only from different places, but from the different places that you yourself are.

There is the place where you are.

Then, there are other places, where you think that everything else is.

Now for me—you are leading me to the topic that worries me most, that has always worried me—the feeling of wondering whether we really exist, or whether the world is a reflection of ourselves. If you are here because I'm thinking of you, if you are here because in this moment I am imagining you along with everything else that exists, then I'm alone in the world inventing everything that exists, imagining everything that is happening, creating the world. When I was a teenager, I experienced this sensation very intensely, and it made me horribly anxious. Because it's unbearable to live with this feeling, this idea that other people aren't really there, that instead they live only in the world that you are imagining, and your eyes are the ones that are seeing that image. Then, you feel that the whole world is inside you. I believe that solipsism is this type of aberration. It's a philosophical position, but a very bitter one. Where is that place located, that inside and outside? Well, these topological issues seem to be exactly what most concern me, you know? It seems that my own problem is embodied in the Möbius strip. I don't know if I'm on the inside or the outside.

No one knows the answer to this question. If I close my eyes, the world disappears. I just have to close them, and then you disappear, this disappears, that disappears. That is, if I can't touch you, because, well, with shut eyes I can still touch you, but if I close my eyes and also lose my sense of touch, there you go, if I can't hear you. It's horrible because I think that you are eternally making and unmaking, making and remaking the world.

I know that you have translated Emily Dickinson. How has the experience of translating another poetic language been for you?

It's a pity that I can't answer more than a portion of that question, as my knowledge of English is limited. It's very difficult to obtain this kind of encounter with another language.

Soon after going to the United States—this was a while ago—I managed to bring all of her work back here to Montevideo, and with the little English I knew, I managed to translate fifty poems. An English professor informed me that the most difficult thing about Emily Dickinson isn't necessarily translating her, but understanding her. And I told him that I saw her as a poet with whom I shared many affinities. I knew I understood her meaning and that I could translate her. With the dictionary I managed to learn about who she is, what kind of person she is. I feel like I can translate her because I sense a kindred spirit. She could be my sister. Sometimes she seems like someone who could be at home with us, running around here and there. And, every little thing has meaning in her constant search for transcendence.

Anyway, I lost those fifty poems. I think they were decently translated, but I lost them on a trip where someone else was handling my things. I also had a lovely prologue which spoke precisely of her writing, her lack of punctuation. She uses few periods and commas; she prefers the dash. It felt like a great discovery about her writing, the day when I realized that in her poetry these dashes signified the places where mystery is made. There is the silence that separates one thing from another, but they are united in the background. And those dashes leave you floating in the air. I began to do an analysis of the dashes in Emily Dickinson's poetry. Her work is always on my mind.

"We are always in danger of magic"—this is one of her key phrases.

I'd like it if you could tell me something about the dashes and use of punctuation that occurs in Dickinson.

What happens is that you read a line and suddenly there's a dash where there should be a comma. But, the dash isn't a comma, and it isn't a semicolon. It's just a kind of distance within the statement that Dickinson is making, a pause that simultaneously connects phrases and separates them from each other.

Is it a silence?

No, it's not a silence because the poem goes on. It's something that grows. It's as if she'd suddenly taken a little leap, arriving at a higher level. It's something that ascends, each time making itself more complete, but never reaching completion. This is what the dash contains, wouldn't you say?

All these forms, that are and are not, are the ones that most excite me. Dickinson's use of the dash seems to be the most original. I don't know if other poets from her time worked in this way. I know too little about other writers' original work to be able to comment.

Does she use dashes in order to indicate a subordinate clause?

No, only to continue the clause. She writes one thing. Yes, she is relating everything to everything else. I understand this because I tend to do it as well.

Have you applied this to your own writing?

I have started applying it. When I started using slashes, obliques, instead of dashes, I should have been using dashes.

Does the oblique have the same intention?

The oblique has a little of that. It's not exactly the same, but it's similar.

And what might the intention be?

The oblique is a mode... I feel as if there were a kind of... well, the word "mystery" is very strong, but it feels like a kind of unknown thing, a place where you have to stop. Sometimes, reading those poems, one has the tendency to keep reading as if the lines were connected, and they're not. A line, a dash demands respect due to its vision, its mode. Because it has a special power.

Now, you'll see that Juan Gelman[3] uses dashes quite a lot, and it seems to me that he uses them very well. And he uses them in this way. It's a way of going on and not going on. It's totally strange. In my opinion, all the classic forms of punctuation have been used up; they seem to belong to a very ordinary form of language.

Do you think the dash relates to the caesura, for example?

Well, the caesura is more natural. It's a kind of chord in the language that comes about completely naturally. And you can easily spot it whether it's marked by punctuation or not—it's just right there. But with the dash it's different; suddenly it's a single word that you are dividing. You don't allow for any alteration of the rhythm, any change in the number of syllables. In addition to that, you see, there is the whole phenomenon of internal rhymes. I think it's fairly natural for the writer to use these. In terms of my personal experience, words are joined sometimes due to sounds or endings. I would be able to join a series of words even though they don't have anything to do with each other. One thing that I liked a lot was to start speaking in an octosyllabic way, even if I ended up with meaningless but well-placed rhymes. It's a good exercise to try. There's something that pushes you and guides you; the words keep coming and coming based on their common sound. When you find the rhyme, you begin to link words together, and they come, they keep coming.

What sequence would you make with mystery, secret, and silence?

Well, these three things are not exactly the same; the three signify different ideas. Silence is a mystery. A mystery is a secret. But they change according to the position you give them, don't they? Like a molecular structure. That thing science has of mystery, in that for every change you make, the structure is transformed into something else. The total change of structure! Just based

---

3   Juan Gelman (1930-2014), a major Argentine poet, is most well-known for his poetic resistance to the dictatorship of the 1970s and the Dirty War.

on the positioning! This reminds me of that other phrase I love and have repeated ever since I first heard it: "The table, that mad dance of electrons."

Do you think that written poetry runs the risk of disappearing due to new forms of communication?

How many times I've thought about this! And sometimes I reach the conclusion that no, even with everything that's happening, poetry cannot disappear. That is to say, I believe that there will always be a possibility of communicating with a mark, a color, the feeling that you have to leave a footprint. It can be a letter of the alphabet, a note, a mathematical sign. Books may change; they might come to assume another form entirely... One of my central themes is that of metamorphosis. I always feel that from birth to death we are constantly changing. Everything changes. The cells of the body, letters, words, customs, ages... Everything changes.

Would you say that this metamorphosis is related to the nature of time?

Time's passing is a transformation. I always remember a quote from the eighteenth century scientist Lavoisier, who stated, "Nothing is created, nothing is destroyed, everything is transformed." I always feel this change— in the body, in the hours, in the day, in all things. When you become conscious of all this, especially when you've reached a certain age, you start to see that the whole world works this way. It's as if it were a great mass that were constantly changing itself, constantly transforming itself into something else. Therefore I don't know which way we will go, and sometimes I have to ask myself... Are robots our future? The ultimate metamorphosis? Where will we end up? Perhaps pieces of our hearts, our brains, are already beginning to change? But there is something fundamental that does not change, and that is poetry. I have to wonder why it is that we can read a poem of Sappho or Omar Khayyam, translated from a language that we don't understand, and still we are excited by it. It seems like there is some kind of central thread within the very evolution of man, where poetry is the only thing that has managed to preserve itself, to relate.

What does one need in order to write?

There is one thing that is indeed necessary: the need itself, the need for expression.

Do you have an invisible reader?

She's not invisible; she's in the future, a ghost. I call her the ghost reader. In the future, always in the future. Never now, always later. So, in one sense I always know what's ahead of me. Further ahead.

About the Editors

Kristin Dykstra is principal translator of *The Winter Garden Photograph*, by Reina María Rodríguez, forthcoming from Ugly Duckling Presse (with some co-translations by Nancy Gates Madsen). She is the translator of *Cubanology*, a book of days by Omar Pérez (Station Hill Press), and *Other Letters to Milena*, a mixed-genre book by Reina María Rodríguez published by University of Alabama Press, which has also published her translations of Cuban authors Juan Carlos Flores, Angel Escobar, and Marcelo Morales. She is guest editor of a dossier dedicated to Flores (1962–2016) in *Chicago Review*. The recipient of an NEA Literary Translation Fellowship, Dykstra won the inaugural Gulf Coast Prize for Literary Translation.

Kent Johnson lived and worked for many years in Costa Rica, Uruguay, and Nicaragua. With Michael Boughn, he manages the web journal *Dispatches from the Poetry Wars*. Author, translator, or editor of more than thirty titles in relation to poetry, he is most recently co-editor of the anthology *Resist Much/Obey Little: Inaugural Poems to the Resistance* and author of *Homage to the Pseudo-Avant-Garde*. In 2015, UDP released a pamphlet of his annotated translation of César Vallejo's only known interview.

About the Contributors

Roberto Echavarren is an award-winning poet, novelist, essayist, playwright and translator from Uruguay. Among his many poetry collections are *Centralasia, El expreso entre el sueño y la vigilia* (The express between sleep and wakefulness) and *Ruido de fondo* (Background Noise). Echavarren is co-director of La Flauta Mágica publishing company, specializing in critical bilingual editions of poetry and the rescue of major poetic works written in Spanish.

Silvia Guerra has published many books of poetry, among them *Estampas de un tapiz, Nada de nadie, La sombra de la azucena, Replicantes Astrales, Idea de la aventura,* and *De la arena nace el agua*. She is also the author of a prose biography of Lautréamont, *Fuera del relato*. With Chilean poet Verónica Zondek, Guerra coedited two books featuring Gabriela Mistral and her connections with Uruguayan writers. Guerra has helped to organize the Primer Festival Hispanoamericano de Poesía in Uruguay and co-directs La Flauta Mágica with Roberto Echavarren.

About the Translators

Gillian Brassil studied translation at Brown University and was the recipient of a Fulbright fellowship in Madrid in 2012. She lives in Brooklyn and works for a production company in Santa Fe, New Mexico. She also freelances as a writer, fact-checker, and translator.

Anna Deeny Morales is a translator, literary critic, and dramatist. She has translated works by Raúl Zurita, Mercedes Roffé, and Alejandra Pizarnik, among others. Original works for contemporary dance and theater include *La straniera* and *Tela di Ragno*, as well as adaptations of *zarzuelas*, *Cecilia Valdés* and *La Verbena de la Paloma*. She is the winner of an NEA fellowship for the translation of *Tala* by Gabriela Mistral. She received a doctoral degree from the University of California, Berkeley, and teaches at Georgetown University.

Mónica de la Torre is the author of six books of poetry, including *The Happy End/All Welcome* (UDP) and *Feliz año nuevo*, a volume of selected poetry published in Spain (Luces de Gálibo). Born and raised in Mexico City, she writes in, and translates into, Spanish and English. She teaches in the Literary Arts program at Brown University.

Urayoán Noel is the author of the critical study *In Visible Movement: Nuyorican Poetry from the Sixties to Slam* (Iowa) and six books of poetry, most recently *Buzzing Hemisphere/Rumor Hemisférico* (Arizona). His translations include *No Budu Please* by Wingston González (UDP) and *Architecture of Dispersed Life: Selected Poetry* by Pablo de Rokha (Shearsman). Originally from Puerto Rico, Noel lives in the Bronx and teaches at NYU, as well as at Stetson University's MFA of the Americas.

Jeannine Marie Pitas is a writer, teacher, and Spanish-English literary translator currently living in Dubuque, Iowa, where she teaches at the University of Dubuque. She is the author of two poetry chapbooks and the translator of several Uruguayan poets. She has published translations of acclaimed Uruguayan writer Marosa di Giorgio's work, *The History of Violets* and *I Remember Nightfall* (UDP), and her own first full-length poetry collection, *Things Seen and Unseen*, is forthcoming from Mosaic Press.

Alex Verdolini is a Ph.D. candidate in the Department of Comparative Literature at Yale University. Recent essays and translations have appeared in publications such as *MLN*, *The Brooklyn Rail*, *Mandorla*, *Inventory*, and *6x6*.

The Lost Literature Series from Ugly Duckling Presse